Hiking & Mountain Biking
Pisgah Forest

Jim Parham

milestone
press

almond, nc

Copyright 2016 by Jim Parham
All rights reserved
Second printing April 2018

Milestone Press, P.O. Box 158, Almond, NC 28702
www.milestonepress.com

Book design by Jim Parham

Cover photographs by Jim Parham and Mary Ellen Hammond.
Interior photographs by the author except as follows.
Mary Ellen Hammond: pp. 15, 38, 112-116, 192.

Library of Congress Cataloging-in-Publication Data

Names: Parham, Jim.
Title: Hiking & mountain biking Pisgah Forest / Jim Parham.
Description: Almond, NC : Milestone Press, [2016]
Identifiers: LCCN 2016000050 | ISBN 9781889596341
   (alk. paper)
Subjects: LCSH: Hiking–North Carolina–Pisgah National
   Forest–Guidebooks. | Mountain biking–North Carolina–Pisgah
   National Forest–Guidebooks. | Trails–North Carolina–Pisgah
   National Forest–Guidebooks. | Pisgah National Forest (N.C.)–
   Guidebooks.
Classification: LCC GV199.42.N66 P38 2016 | DDC
796.5109756–dc23
LC record available at http://lccn.loc.gov/2016000050

Printed on recycled paper in the United States of America

*This book is sold with the understanding that the author and
publisher assume no legal responsibility for the completeness or
accuracy of the contents of this book, nor for any damages,
including injury and loss of life, incurred while attempting any of
the activities or visiting any of the destinations described within it.
The text is based on information available at the time of publication.*

Table of Contents

Overnight Hike Routes

Mountain Bike Routes

Table of Contents (continued)

Mountain Biking Routes (continued)

Waterfalls

Appendices

Pisgah District

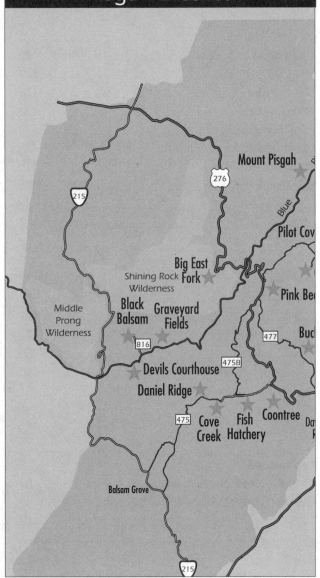

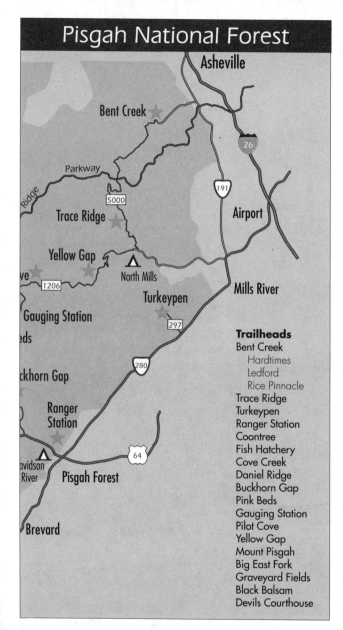

Pisgah National Forest

Asheville

Bent Creek ★

26

Parkway

Ridge

5000

191

Trace Ridge ★

Airport

Yellow Gap ★

1206

△
North Mills

Mills River

Turkeypen

297

Gauging Station

eds

280

ckhorn Gap

Ranger
Station ★

64

△
avidson
River

Pisgah Forest

Brevard

Trailheads
Bent Creek
  Hardtimes
  Ledford
  Rice Pinnacle
Trace Ridge
Turkeypen
Ranger Station
Coontree
Fish Hatchery
Cove Creek
Daniel Ridge
Buckhorn Gap
Pink Beds
Gauging Station
Pilot Cove
Yellow Gap
Mount Pisgah
Big East Fork
Graveyard Fields
Black Balsam
Devils Courthouse

Overview Map

Introduction

The Pisgah District of the Pisgah National Forest is one of the East Coast's most popular outdoor recreation destinations. This huge chunk of rugged land straddles the Blue Ridge Parkway just to the southeast of Asheville, western North Carolina's largest town. Most folks just call it Pisgah. The scenery here is as dramatic as it gets. Sheer rock cliffs—for example, Looking Glass Rock, John Rock, and Cedar Rock—stand like sentinels, rising out of the craggy terrain. In the highest realms, you'll find peaks that rise to over 6,000 feet where the air is cool even on the hottest of summer days. Down in the valleys, clear, cold streams cascade over waterfalls and through lush rhododendron tangles. Wildflowers bloom most everywhere and in all seasons except the coldest winter months. It's a beautiful place you'll want to visit time and time again.

You'd never know it now, but before the turn of the 20th century this land was completely logged out. The hillsides green with trees today were then barren and covered with slash piles, eroding away and mucking up the waterways. It looked as if it were beyond hope. Along came a man named George W. Vanderbilt—a dandy from New York with a railroad fortune's worth of money to spend. Starting in 1889, Vanderbilt began buying up most of the land we know today as Pisgah, hired a professional forester named Carl Schenck, and then did something remarkable. He completely reclaimed the landscape—and in doing so created the first school of forestry in United States. That school led to the birth of the U.S. Forest Service, and Pisgah became our nation's first national forest.

Pisgah is All About Trails

It's not just the scenery that makes this such a great destination for day hikers, backpackers, and mountain bikers; the area also boasts over 350 miles of single track trails and hundreds more miles of gated forest roads. It's the largest concentration of trails open to both hikers and cyclists in the entire Southeast. The trails are well marked with signs and blazes and the gated roads are marked by number. All of these trails and roads are easily accessible, some by paved roads, others by well-maintained gravel roads. A number of the trailheads feature large, paved parking lots with picnic tables and toilet facilities; others are small turnouts suitable for a handful of cars. You'll have no trouble getting around and finding your trail for the day.

Day hikers looking for a day or half-day outing have any number of routes to choose from. You can hike to the highest summits, stroll through tunnels of mountain laurel and flame azalea, or seek out a hidden waterfall. In these pages you'll find 20 of the best day hikes in Pisgah. Choose one, or when you've done them all, use the maps to make up your own.

Backpacking in Pisgah is awesome. It's as if the builders had overnight hiking in mind when they created the trail system. With so many streams and rivers, finding spots near water to camp is a piece of cake. Your home for the night might be near a mountain spring, a melodious babbling brook, or even a splashing waterfall. Head up into the higher elevations and sleeping under the stars becomes more than a euphemism; the lack of humidity up there creates an ideal night sky. Listed here are 12 overnight hiking routes plus the two long distance trails of Pisgah. Some are appropriate for just one night out while others work well for two, three, or a week of nights in the woods.

Mountain bikers heading to Pisgah will find every kind of trail route imaginable. Beginner riders can choose from a number of easier trails linked with gated forest roads to make fine loops. Cyclists with more experience will want to branch out to the somewhat more rugged trails. Pisgah is great for using a gated road to make your climb and then turning to a series of trails to bring you back down to your car. Expert riders will find more challenge than they could ever hope for: long single track climbs,

A father-son moment high on the Mountains-to-Sea Trail.

rocky, log-hopping descents, waist-deep river crossings, clifftop views, and enough trail mileage to do all-day epic rides. Note that due to the ruggedness of the terrain, the trails in Pisgah are significantly more difficult than other trails in the Southeast. This guide lists a total of 29 routes for mountain bikers to choose from.

Land of Waterfalls

If you run into someone wandering around in the woods in Pisgah with a sketchy-looking map in hand and a questioning look on his or her face, chances are s/he is looking for a waterfall. The area is billed as the land of waterfalls, and most all the tourist establishments have brochures with directions in some form or another, which they use both to attract people to their establishment and help them find a waterfall or two. Many of the hikes and bike rides in this book will take you past one or more waterfalls. They are excellent places to hang out, swim, eat a snack, or just relax in the woods. If heading straight to a waterfall is your goal (whether on foot, by car, or on a bike), you'll also find in this guide separate directions to 21 of Pisgah's waterfalls.

When to Go

When's the best time to go hiking, biking, and camping in Pisgah? Most anytime of the year is good. Summers can be hot—in the 80s—but the temperature really depends on the elevation of your destination. Trails up high around the Blue Ridge Parkway tend to be around 10 degrees cooler than those down around the ranger station or in Bent Creek. Your biggest threat this time of year is afternoon thunderstorms. They don't call it Pisgah National "rain forest" for nothing. Expect it to rain at some point at some place in Pisgah most any day of the summer—and be glad when it's dry. Spring and fall weather is almost always ideal. You'll experience cool, crisp nights and very pleasant, often sunny days. Winters in western North Carolina tend to be mild, but again it really depends on the elevation of your destination. Much of the Blue Ridge Parkway is closed from near the end of November to sometime in March, so access to those high-elevation trailheads by car is not possible. If you start low and head high, be prepared for full-on winter weather. Lower down, it can be really pleasant on a winter day. Always check the forecast ahead of time, dress accordingly, and regardless of the time of year be sure to include a rain jacket and lightweight warm upper layer in your kit.

What follows in this pocket guide is the bare-bones essential information to get you out of your house and into the woods of Pisgah, whether it be on a bicycle or your own two feet. You'll find maps and directions to get you first to the trailhead and then away on the route itself. It's small enough to slide right into an outside pocket where the information is easily accessible. Refer to it as necessary, and then tuck it away. Open your eyes, breathe deep, and enjoy the full experience of the mountains of Pisgah.

Important Considerations

Waterfalls

Every year people die at waterfalls, and some have died at waterfalls listed in this book. Here's what usually happens. They try to climb up the cliff or steep slope beside a waterfall to get a better view or take a picture or make an attempt to reach the top, and then they slip and fall. They try to peer over the edge at the top, and then they slip and fall. They try to climb the waterfall itself, and then they slip and fall. Everything near a waterfall—rocks, roots, fallen trees—is wet and slippery. If you do any of these things, it's only a matter of time before you slip and fall, too. At best you'll twist an ankle or break an arm; at worst it could be fatal. Certainly your mistake will ruin what could have been a nice outing for you and everyone else. *Always exercise extreme caution and common sense around waterfalls.*

Rules of the Trail

Hikers
- Hikers yield to horses. Step off the trail.
- Keep dogs under control, especially when encountering other hikers, mountain bikers or horses; horses can easily be startled by barking dogs.
- Though trail etiquette dictates that bikers yield to you, keep your ears open—especially when hiking up hill. If you hear a cyclist rattling down, chances are he will not be able to stop. In this case, it's best if you step off the trail.

Bikers

- Bikers yield to all other trail users.
- Ride within your skill level and stay in control.
- Always wear a helmet.
- When approaching horses, dismount your bike and ask the riders how they would like you to proceed.
- Carry a spare tube, pump and basic tool kit.

Swimming

Swimming is allowed pretty much anywhere in Pisgah. Use your best judgment and swim at your own risk— there are no lifeguards.

Exposed Rock Outcrops

Be especially careful around the tops of cliffs. In many places, vantage viewpoints are right on the top edge of a sloping rock face. These sites tend to slope downward with increasing angulature. Stay well back from the edge as the rock is often extremely slippery, even if it has not rained in a while.

Cell Phones

Cell phones do not work in most parts of the forest. You might get lucky on a high ridge or from an overlook. In an emergency, you can always try for a signal and maybe you can get out a text. However, it's better to assume you won't be able to use your phone; don't put yourself in a situation where you need to rely on coverage.

Wildlife

When it comes to wildlife in Pisgah, it basically boils down to the critters you probably want to see and the critters you most likely don't want to see.

How to see wildlife

The chances of you spotting wildlife while out on the trail are pretty good, but there are things you can do to increase your chances in Pisgah. Though accustomed to people, the birds, deer, turkey, squirrels, snakes, and other animals there do their best to avoid you, especially when you are in a crowd or making lots of noise. If you find you've been on your own or in a small group for a while, slow down and get quiet. You may even want to head off the trail a bit, find a log or a big rock, and just sit quietly. You'll be surprised how quickly the forest comes alive with the sights and sounds of animal life.

Wild turkey are a common sight in Pisgah.

Another tactic is to head out on the trail just after dawn or just before dusk. Many animals are out and about this time of day to feed. They also know that many of the humans have called it quits for the day. Walk around quietly and see what you see.

Birding

The varied terrain and sheer size of the forest means Pisgah is a good place to see birds of all types. If a species is listed in a birding guide for these mountains, chances are you'll see or hear it flitting around somewhere near to a trail. There are some notables you might want to look for. The cliffs of Looking Glass Rock and Devil's Courthouse are home to peregrine falcons; look for them early in the morning, soaring on the thermals. Head up to the Blue Ridge Parkway or one of the 6,000-footers sometime in late September for the annual hawk migration. It's a thrill to count these birds as they fly over, heading south.

Wildlife to look out for

Along with all the warm and fuzzy creatures in the woods are the ones you'd just as soon avoid. Usually people tend to first think, *Bears!* and then, *Snakes!* Sure, you might be fearful of these and seek to avoid contact, but the creatures that usually cause the most problems in the forest are yellow jackets and hornets. Encountering either of these can quickly turn a peaceful walk or bike ride in the mountains into a complete panic, with people running pell-mell through the woods screaming and tearing their clothes off—it happens. Those stings can hurt like the dickens, and for anyone who is severely allergic they can be deadly. Hornets like to build their gray, football-shaped nests over water, so be especially careful around creeks and streams. Yellow jackets build their nests in the ground—sometimes right in the middle of the trail. Be cautious of insects flying in and out of quarter-sized openings in the ground. If you see a cloud of them hovering over such a hole, know they're aggravated and give them a wide berth.

Hunting season

During the fall and on select spring dates, if you're hiking in the national forest there's a chance you'll run into game hunters. Most of the time, especially during small game season, this is not a problem. However, on opening day of rifle deer hunting season, around major holidays, and during bear season, it can be a big deal. On these days, in some places, it can seem that the woods are full of hunters—and you might not be comfortable with that. Regardless, it's a good idea to wear bright colors in the woods during hunting seasons. For specific hunting dates in North Carolina check the website at ncwildlife.org.

Wildflowers

The woods, fields, streams, waterfalls, and cliff areas of Pisgah are prime habitat for many species of wildflowers throughout the spring summer and fall.

Wildflower folks fall into two camps: those who like to head off on any trail, any time of the year and just see what they see, and those who like to go in search of a particular flower—the rarer the better. If you fall into the first group, you'll rarely be disappointed in Pisgah. Spring bursts forth with a variety of ephemerals, those early-blooming herbs seeking the sunshine on the warm forest floor before leaf-out cools things down. Heading into early summer, flame azaleas and mountain laurels brighten the hillsides, soon to be followed by rhododendron along the streams. In late summer, you might see cardinal flower growing in the boulders at the water's edge. Before you know it, the year slips into fall and you're spotting giant Joe-pye weed in the fields and gentians in the woods. Arm yourself with a good fieldguide and head off on a trail.

If you're in the second camp, there are some flowers in Pisgah you won't want to miss. Take a walk around the Pink Beds in mid-April and if you are lucky you might see a bed of swamp pinks—the Pink Beds' namesake flower. These rare, waist-high lilies are a sight to see. In May you can go up around Graveyard Fields in search of another seldom-seen pink flower, the exquisite pinkshell azalea. So abundant are they there and along the Blue Ridge Parkway near Devil's Courthouse, you'd never guess that North Carolina lists them as significantly rare.

Planning Your Trip

What to Expect

It's a good idea to carry basic backcountry provisions when on an outing in Pisgah Forest. The following gear lists will go a long way toward keeping you safe and comfortable; nothing can ruin a good hike or bike ride quicker than leaving something essential behind. Remember the Scout motto? Be prepared. Here is a checklist for the various activities.

Day Hikers

Footwear
- comfortable hiking boots or shoes
- woolen or synthetic socks that fit well (no cotton)

Outerwear (be prepared to add layers; no cotton shirts or jeans)
- shorts or light pants and quick-dry t-shirt (your base layer)
- cap or wide-brimmed hat
- neon or bright orange vest (in hunting season)

In Your Daypack
- lunch/high-energy snacks
- water (2 liters per person)
- insect repellent
- personal first-aid kit
- sunscreen and lip balm
- rain jacket (always)
- long-sleeved shirt (always)

- emergency flashlight
- map and/or guidebook
- small plastic trash bag

Nice To Have
- walking stick or trekking poles
- pocket knife or multi-tool
- camera

Overnight Backpackers

To Carry
- backpack
- sleeping bag
- sleeping pad
- shelter
- stove & fuel, with matches or lighter
- cook pot(s)
- food
- food storage system
- eating utensils
- water container
- water purification system
- headlamp or flashlight
- pocket knife
- first aid kit
- map/guidebook
- extra clothes (see To Wear, below)
- large, heavy-duty plastic bag

Optional
- trekking poles
- pack cover
- camera
- phone
- GPS
- camp chair
- bandana
- insect repellent

To Wear (this is your base layer; no cotton anything)
- footwear
- synthetic or woolen-blend hiking socks
- shorts or light pants
- quick-dry t-shirt (woolen or synthetic)
- cap or wide-brimmed hat

Add
- long-sleeved synthetic shirt
- fleece or wind shirt
- rain jacket & pants
- light gloves
- warm hat

Optional
- sunglasses
- neon or bright orange vest (hunting season)

Mountain Bikers

Footwear
- comfortable bike trail shoes that fit your pedals
- woolen or synthetic socks that fit well (no cotton)

Outerwear (be prepared to add layers; no cotton anything)
- bike shorts and/or bike tights and quick-dry bike jersey
- appropriate ANSI-approved helmet
- bike gloves
- eye protection
- neon or bright orange vest (hunting season)

In Your Hydration Pack

- lunch/high-energy snacks
- water (2+ liters per person; consider carrying a water filter for epic rides)
- insect repellent
- personal first-aid kit
- sunscreen and lip balm
- rain jacket (regardless of the weather)
- map and/or guidebook
- small plastic trash bag
- bike tire pump that fits your tubes
- tube patch kit
- bike repair multi-tool
- spare tubes that fit your wheels

Getting to Pisgah & the Trailheads

The Pisgah District of the Pisgah National Forest is easy to get to no matter which direction you're coming from. The following driving directions are to the Pisgah District Ranger Station and Visitors Center located just north of the town of Pisgah Forest on US 276, open daily from 9 am to 5 pm.

Pisgah District Ranger Station
1600 Pisgah Hwy
Pisgah Forest, NC 28768
828-682-6146
GPS 35.284739, -82.726621

From Brevard/Pisgah Forest, NC
1. Drive north on US 276 a short distance into the Forest.
2. The ranger station and visitor center will be on your right just past the entrance to Davidson River Campground.

From Hendersonville, NC
1. Drive north on US 64 to the town of Pisgah Forest.
2. At the intersection with US 276 continue straight onto US 276 and head into the national forest; the visitor center will be on your right just past the entrance to Davidson River Campground.

From Asheville, NC
1. Take I-26 south to Asheville Regional Airport (exit 40).
2. Turn right (south) on NC 280.

3. In Mills River, turn left (south) to remain on NC 280.
4. At the intersection with US 276/64 in the town of Pisgah Forest, turn right (north) onto US 276 to head into the national forest; the visitor center will be on your right just past the entrance to Davidson River Campground.

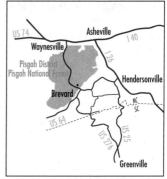

From the North Carolina side of the Great Smoky Mountains

1. Take US 74 east to Waynesville.
2. Turn right (south) on US 276 to travel over the mountains, crossing the Blue Ridge Parkway, through the heart of the Pisgah District, and down to the edge of the forest where the ranger station will be on your left.

From Greenville, SC

1. Drive north on US 276, passing through the towns of Travelers Rest, Marietta, and Cleveland.
2. Once past Cleveland, at the intersection of US 276 and SC 11, turn right on US 276 towards Caesars Head.
3. Drive on US 276 up and over Caesars Head, passing the SC-NC state line, and continue all the way to Brevard.
4. In Brevard, turn right to stay on US 276/64 to the town of Pisgah Forest.
5. When US 276 and US 64 diverge in the town of Pisgah Forest, turn left (north) to continue on US 276. Head into the national forest; the visitor center will be on your right, just past the entrance to Davidson River Campground.

Directions to the Trailheads

All the hikes and mountain bike routes in this guide begin at one of the 18 trailheads listed below. The majority of these have plenty of parking; those with the least space can still accommodate 5 or 6 cars. The seven largest have toilets (although the toilets might be portable or pit-style).

Directions are given from the Pisgah District Ranger Station and Visitor Center.

Bent Creek (Three trailheads close together)
Rice Pinnacle   GPS 35.496523, -82.615826
Hardtimes   GPS 35.487931, -82.623978
Ledford Branch   GPS 35.496517, -82.615757

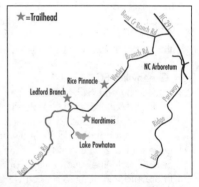

1. From the ranger station parking lot, turn left on US 276 and head south out of the national forest.
2. Turn left on NC 280 in Pisgah Forest.
3. Turn left NC 191 in Mills River.
4. Just after passing under the Blue Ridge Parkway. Turn left on Wesley Branch Road toward Lake Powhatan.
5. Just after passing the NC Arboretum look for Rice Pinnacle trailhead on the right. Soon after that is Hardtimes trailhead on the left, and finally Ledford trailhead on the right.

Trace Ridge
GPS 35.420406,
-82.656772

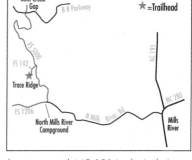

1. From the ranger station parking lot, turn left on US 276 and head south out of the national forest.
2. Turn left on NC 280 in Pisgah Forest.
3. In Mills River, just before the junction with NC 191 (at the Ingles), turn left on North Mills River Road.
4. When you reach North Mills River Campground, turn right on FS 5000.
5. Drive 2.1 miles and turn left on FS 142.
6. Continue another 0.5 mile to Trace Ridge trailhead.

Turkeypen Gap
GPS 35.342954,
-82.659246

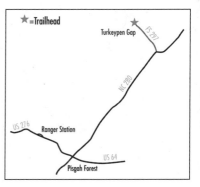

1. From the ranger station parking lot, turn left on US 276 and head south out of the national forest.
2. Turn left on NC 280 in Pisgah Forest.
3. Continue 5.0 miles and turn left on Turkeypen Gap Road (FS 297).
3. Turkeypen Gap trailhead is at the end of this road.

Ranger Station (Black Mountain)
GPS 35.283708, -82.722826

1. From the ranger station parking lot, turn left on US 276.
2. Drive a very short distance and turn left into the parking area just past the maintenance shed.

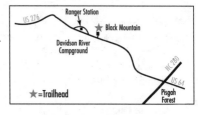

3. This is the trailhead for Black Mountain Trail.

Coontree
GPS 35.289430, -82.762236

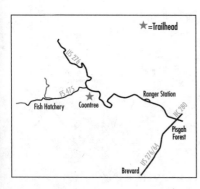

1. From the ranger station parking lot, turn right onto US 276.
2. Continue for 3.3 miles and park at Coontree Picnic Area, on the left.

Looking Glass Rock
GPS 35.291200, -82.776550

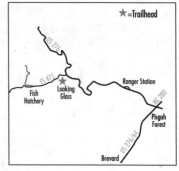

1. From the ranger station parking lot, turn right on US 276.
2. Continue north for 3.7 miles and turn left, following signs for Pisgah Fish Hatchery and Wildlife Education Center.

3. In 0.4 mile you'll see the trailhead parking beside the road on the left, across from Looking Glass Trail.

Fish Hatchery
GPS 35.284604, -82.791849

1. From the ranger station parking lot, turn right on US 276.
2. Continue on US 276 north for 3.7 miles and turn left, following signs for Pisgah Fish Hatchery and Wildlife Education Center.
3. Drive 1.5 miles and turn left into the very large fish hatchery parking area.

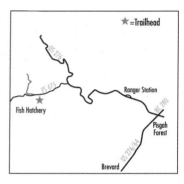

Cove Creek
GPS 35.282750, -82.816469

1. From the ranger station parking lot, turn right on US 276.
2. Continue north for 3.7 miles and turn left, following signs for Pisgah Fish Hatchery and Wildlife Education Center.
3. Continue past the fish hatchery on paved FS 475 up and over the hill.
4. Park where the road turns to gravel in the small lot just across from the entrance to Cove Creek Group Camp.

Daniel Ridge
GPS 35.284804, -82.829169

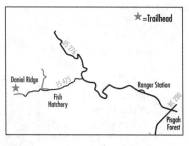

1. From the ranger station parking lot, turn right on US 276.
2. Continue on US 276 north for 3.7 miles and turn left, following the signs for Pisgah Fish Hatchery and Wildlife Education Center.
3. Continue past the fish hatchery on paved FS 475 up and over the hill.
4. At the entrance to Cove Creek Group Camp the road turns to gravel. Continue another 0.5 mile.
5. Reach the parking area for Daniel Ridge. It's on the right.

Buckhorn Gap
GPS 35.316462, -82.752304

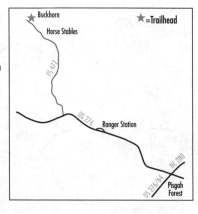

1. From the ranger station parking lot, turn right on US 276.
2. Continue on US 276 north for 0.5 mile and turn right on FS 477.
3. Continue another 2.3 miles to the Buckhorn Gap trailhead on the right.

Pink Beds
GPS 35.353312, -82.778977

1. From the ranger station parking lot, turn right on US 276.
2. Continue on US 276 north for 11.6 miles to the Pink Beds parking area and picnic area on the right.

Gauging Station
GPS 35.367397, -82.740406

1. From the ranger station parking lot, turn right on US 276.
2. Continue on US 276 north for 12 miles past the Pink Beds parking and picnic area to FS 1206; turn right.
3. Drive 3.3 miles and turn right on FS 476.
4. Continue another 1.4 miles to the Gauging Station parking lot at the end of the road.

Pilot Cove
GPS 35.383382, -82.714882

1. From the ranger station parking lot, turn right on US 276.
2. Continue on US 276 north for 12 miles past the Pink Beds parking and picnic area to FS 1206 and turn right.
4. Drive 4 miles to the Pilot Cove trailhead on the left.

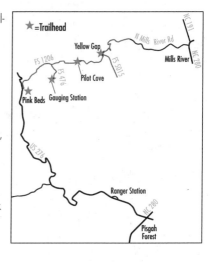

Yellow Gap
GPS 35.394490, -82.676680

1. From the ranger station parking lot, turn right on US 276.
2. Continue on US 276 north for 12 miles past the Pink Beds parking and picnic area to FS 1206 and turn right.
4. Drive 7.8 miles to Yellow Gap. There is a small parking area on the right side of the road where Laurel Mountain Trail begins on the left. A short distance beyond, FS 5015 enters from the right.

Mount Pisgah
GPS 35.418705, -82.747974

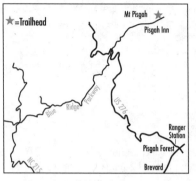

1. From the ranger station parking lot, turn right on US 276.
2. Continue on US 276 north all the way up and turn right (north) on the Blue Ridge Parkway.
3. Pass the Pisgah Inn and at milepost 407.6 turn right into the Buck Springs/Mt. Pisgah parking area. Drive out to the end of the road, which crosses the parkway over a tunnel.

Big East Fork
GPS 35.365675, -82.817969

1. From the ranger station parking lot, turn right on US 276.
2. Continue on US 276 north all the way up to cross under the Blue Ridge Parkway. Turn right (north).
4. Continue another 2.9 miles down to the Big East Fork parking area on the left. Be sure to park in the lot on the far (north) side of the river.

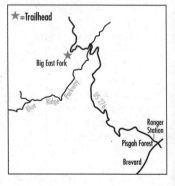

Graveyard Fields
GPS 35.320279, -82.846957

1. From the ranger station parking lot, turn right on US 276.
2. Continue on US 276 north all the way up and turn left (south) on the Blue Ridge Parkway.
3. Continue on to milepost 418.8 to the big parking lot on the right.

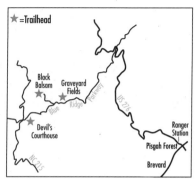

Black Balsam
GPS 35.326048, -82.881868

1. From the ranger station parking lot, turn right on US 276.
2. Continue on US 276 north all the way up and turn left (south) on the Blue Ridge Parkway.
3. Continue on to milepost 420.2 and turn right on FS 816.
4. Park in the lot at the end of the road in 1.3 miles.

Devil's Courthouse
GPS 35.305426, -82.899847

1. From the ranger station parking lot, turn right on US 276.
2. Continue on US 276 north all the way up and turn left (south) on the Blue Ridge Parkway.
3. Continue on to Devil's Courthouse at milepost 422.4.

Navigating Pisgah

The Pisgah District of Pisgah National Forest has hundreds of miles of trails and gated roads with which any number of routes can be put together. The routes described in this book were chosen based on popularity, distance, difficulty, and ease of trail navigation. Trails and roads in Pisgah are well marked with signs, and the trails have blazes of varying colors. The exceptions to this rule are Shining Rock and Middle Prong Wilderness Areas. Here you may see only a rough sign or two as befits designated wilderness. As you hike or mountain bike, double-check all trail intersections and turns, and be sure to carry this guidebook on all your Pisgah adventures. Hiking and biking routes are arranged by trailhead location.

Route Map Legend	
···	Route
- - -	other trail
▬	paved road
—	dirt road
🛁	waterfall
TH	trailhead
P	parking

Route maps accompany each route description. Each map shows the described route as a broken green line. All other roads and trails are shown in black or gray.

Most trail signs are carsonite wands like this one, denoting the trail name, blaze color, and difficulty rating.

HIKING & MOUNTAIN BIKING PISGAH FOREST

Pisgah Forest

Day Hike Routes

Bent Creek–Arboretum

An old concrete bridge crosses Bent Creek.

Distance	4 miles, out and back
Difficulty	Easy
Location	Bent Creek
Time	2 hours
Crowds	Light weekday mornings; heavy weekends and afternoons
Trailhead	Hardtimes

Route Directions	
1	From the back end of the parking lot, walk down the wide gated roadway.
2	After 0.2 mile, turn left when you reach the creek on Old Bent Creek Road.
3	Continue another 0.7 mile and pass through a gate into the NC Arboretum.

| 4 | Wander around in the Arboretum as much as you like. If you stay on Old Bent Creek Road, it 's another mile to the far end of the Arboretum. Various short paths loop off from this road into different gardens. |
| 5 | Return to the trailhead via Old Bent Creek Road the same way you came in. |

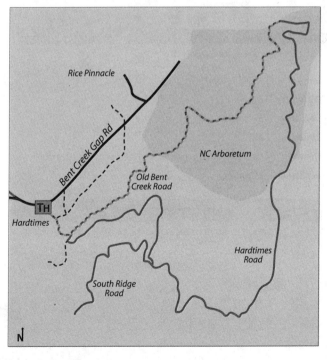

You're likely to see geese on Lake Powhatan.

Distance	4.2-mile loop
Difficulty	Easy
Location	Bent Creek
Time	2 hours
Crowds	Light weekday mornings; heavy weekends and afternoons
Trailhead	Hardtimes

	Route Directions
1	Exit the back end of the parking lot and walk down the wide gated roadway.
2	After 0.2 mile, turn right when you reach the creek on Old Bent Creek Road.
3	Continue 0.1 mile and turn left across Bent Creek on a bridge, then turn right on Homestead Trail (orange blaze).
4	Partway around Lake Powhatan, turn left on Small Creek Trail (red blaze).

5	In 0.3 mile, two trails come in from the left. Go up the steps and straight onto Deerfield Loop Trail (yellow blaze).
6	After another 0.5 mile turn left onto Pine Tree Loop Trail (blue blaze).
7	Circle around on the loop, ignoring trails exiting to the left, to reach a paved road. Turn left on the pavement and then right onto the anglers' access road on the north side of the lake.
8	Cross over the earth hump at the spillway and continue along the creek.
9	Turn left to return to the trailhead the way you came in.

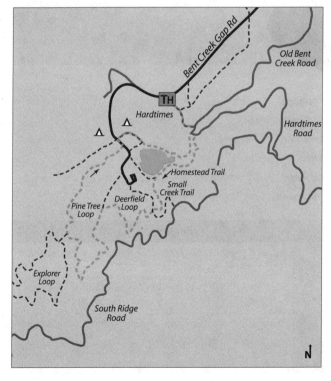

Ledford Gap

The picnic tables at the gap make a great place to take a break.

Distance	3.8-mile loop
Difficulty	Easy
Location	Bent Creek
Time	2 hours
Crowds	Light weekday mornings; heavy weekends and afternoons
Trailhead	Ledford Branch

Route Directions	
1	Walk out of the upper portion of the parking lot, around the gate, and onto FS 479E (Ledford Branch Road).
2	After 0.8 mile of gentle climbing you'll reach Ledford Gap. There are several picnic tables here. FS 479F enters from the left. Continue on FS 479E.
3	Go another 0.6 mile and make a hard right onto Wolf Branch Trail (yellow blaze).
4	Continue down the hill 0.6 mile and turn right to stay on Wolf Branch Trail.
5	Turn right onto Deer Lake Lodge Trail (orange blaze) in 0.8 mile.

6	Intersect a connector trail at a powerline opening. Bear right to stay on Deer Lake Lodge Trail.
7	Remain on Deer Lake Lodge Trail back to the trailhead.

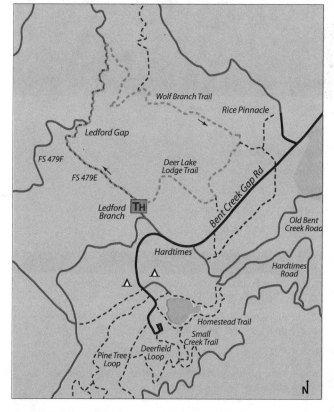

Interpretive signs along the route enlighten you on forest management.

Distance	8.3-mile loop
Difficulty	Moderate
Location	Bent Creek
Time	4 to 5 hours
Crowds	Light to moderate
Trailhead	Ledford Branch

Route Directions	
1	Walk out of the upper portion of the parking lot, around the gate and onto FS 479E (Ledford Branch Road).
2	After 0.8 mile of gentle climbing you'll reach Ledford Gap. There are several picnic tables here. FS 479F enters from the left. Continue on FS 479E.
3	Go another 0.7 mile and make a hard left onto Ingles Field Gap Trail (blue blaze).
4	Follow Ingles Field Gap Trail 1.9 miles to Ingles Field Gap and turn left onto Little Hickory Top Trail (yellow blaze).

5	Descend on Little Hickory Top Trail for 2.5 miles to turn right on FS 479F.
6	Follow FS 479F down the hill to cross Bent Creek Gap Road onto Campground Connector Trail (blue blaze).
7	When you reach the campground, cross onto the anglers' access road.
8	Cross over the earth hump at the spillway and continue down alongside creek.
9	Turn left, pass the Hardtimes trailhead, and walk up the road to Ledford Branch trailhead to finish where you began.

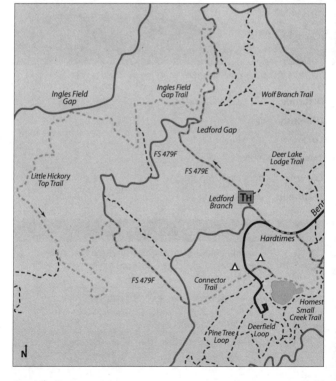

Hendersonville Reservoir

The reservoir holds pure mountain water for the town of Hendersonville.

Distance	2.5 miles, out and back
Difficulty	Easy
Location	Trace Ridge
Time	2 hours
Crowds	Light traffic most days
Trailhead	Trace Ridge

Route Directions	
1	There are two gated roads leaving from the northern end of the trailhead parking area, to the right of the information kiosk. Take the one on the right, heading downhill. This is FS 142.
2	Walk down the road, passing a couple of trails heading off to the left and right. You'll reach the reservoir dam after about 1.3 miles. Spencer Gap Trail circles around to the back of the small lake.
3	After you've seen enough of the lake, return the way you came.

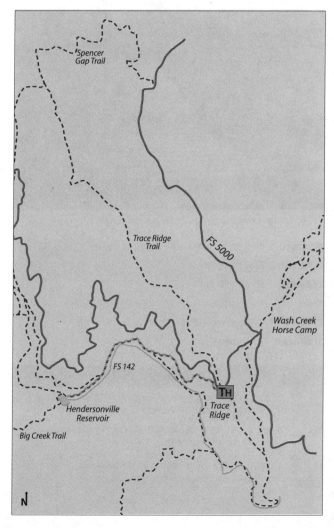

Spencer
Gap Trail

Trace Ridge
Trail

FS 5000

Wash Creek
Horse Camp

FS 142

Hendersonville
Reservoir

TH

Trace
Ridge

Big Creek Trail

N

A series of footbridges take you to the old lodge site.

Distance	8 miles, out and back
Difficulty	Easy to moderate
Location	South Mills River
Time	4 to 6 hours
Crowds	Light on most days
Trailhead	Turkeypen Gap

	Route Directions
1	At the north end of the trailhead parking lot, take South Mills River Trail (white blaze). It starts just to the left of the information kiosk.
2	Continue 0.4 mile to turn left and cross South Mills River on a bouncy, wooden-planked suspension bridge.
3	On the far side of the river the trail goes uphill and away from the river for a short distance before returning to the streambank.

4	A mile or so later you'll cross the second bridge; on the way you will have passed a couple of trails exiting to the right.
5	In just under a mile more you'll cross the third and final suspension bridge.
6	Go another 0.2 mile, cross Cantrell Creek, and arrive at a stone chimney. This is all that's left of Cantrell Creek Lodge at this site. The rest of it was moved and now stands at the Cradle of Forestry.
7	Return to the trailhead the same way you came.

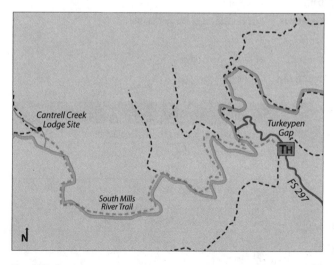

Coontree Loop

Take time to enjoy the creek before you begin your climb up the ridge.

Distance	5-mile loop
Difficulty	Moderate
Location	Just northeast of Ranger Station
Time	3 hours
Crowds	Light on most days
Trailhead	Coontree Picnic Area

Route Directions	
1	Walk across US 276 and onto the Coontree Loop Trail (blue blaze).
2	At 0.2 mile take the left fork of the loop trail and begin a steep climb of more than a mile.
3	Turn left on Bennett Gap Trail (red blaze) and continue another 0.7 mile.
4	Reach a rock outcrop with a great view to the west of Looking Glass Rock. Turn around and retrace your steps back to the loop trail.

5	When you reach the spot where you first turned onto Bennett Gap Trail, continue straight, toward the second junction with Coontree Loop.
6	After another 0.3 mile on Bennett Gap Trail, turn right on Coontree Loop Trail.
7	Go 1.3 miles down the mountain to where the loop began.
8	Bear left, continue 0.2 mile to cross US 276, and finish where you began.

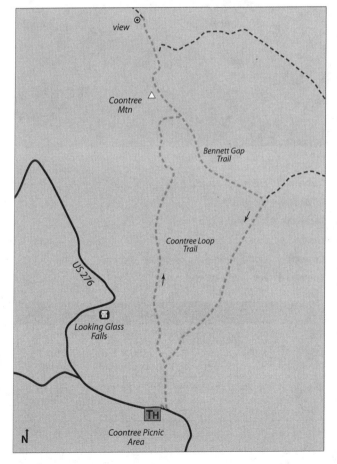

Looking Glass Rock

Looking Glass Rock is a high landmark right in the middle of Pisgah.

Distance	6.2 miles, out and back
Difficulty	Moderate
Location	Just east of Fish Hatchery
Time	3 to 4 hours
Crowds	Light weekdays to moderate weekends
Trailhead	Looking Glass Rock

Route Directions	
1	Looking Glass Rock Trail starts uphill right from the parking lot (blaze yellow).
2	A variety of switchbacks, laurel tunnels, and straight sections for the first 2.3 miles lead to a helicopter landing spot marked by a big H. Keep climbing.
3	At 3.0 miles reach a wide flat spot that marks the top of Looking Glass Rock. There are no views from here. Now begin to descend as you continue along the trail.

| 4 | After 0.1 mile and a drop of 80 ft or so, you'll reach the clifftop views. Be very careful here and stay well away from the more vertical edge. A slip would be catastrophic. |
| 5 | Once you've seen all you want to see, retrace your steps to the trailhead. |

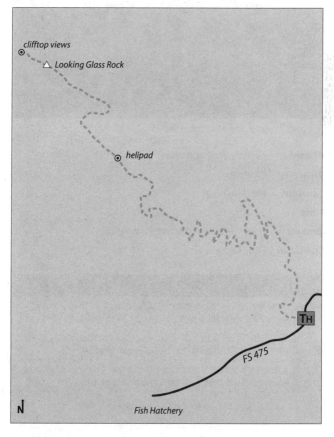

clifftop views

△ Looking Glass Rock

⊙ helipad

TH

FS 475

Fish Hatchery

N

John Rock

It's fun to "hang out on the edge" atop John Rock.

Distance	4.6 miles, out and back
Difficulty	Moderate
Location	Fish Hatchery
Time	3 hours
Crowds	Light weekdays, moderate weekends
Trailhead	Fish Hatchery

Route Directions	
1	Follow the Cat Gap Loop Trail (orange blaze) out of the northeast corner of the large trailhead parking lot. You'll start out close to the Davidson River and then begin climbing.
2	After just over a mile, you'll cross FS 475C, a gated forest road.
3	Several tenths of a mile after crossing the forest road, turn right on John Rock Trail (yellow blaze). The trail continues to climb at about same rate.

| 4 | Not quite a mile more brings you to the clifftop views. John Rock Trail itself steers clear of the clifftop, but you'll see a couple of unmarked trails tunneling through the mountain laurel on your right. Be extremely careful on the rock-faced clifftop; avoid it altogether in wet weather. |
| 5 | After you've enjoyed the views, return the way you came. |

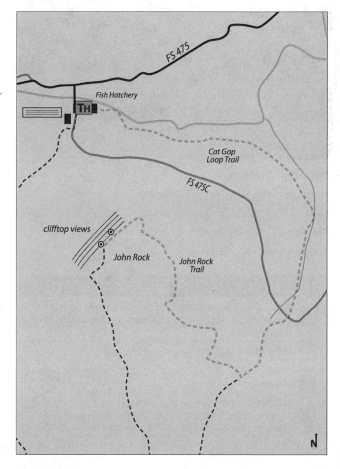

Cat Gap Loop

You'll navigate a few log bridges on the way to Cat Gap.

Distance	4.4-mile loop
Difficulty	Moderate
Location	Fish Hatchery
Time	3 hours
Crowds	Light weekdays, moderate weekends
Trailhead	Fish Hatchery

Route Directions	
1	Follow Cat Gap Loop Trail (orange blaze) out of the northeast corner of the large trailhead parking lot. You'll start out close to the Davidson River and then begin climbing.
2	After just over a mile cross FS 475C, a gated forest road.
3	Farther along, pass the John Rock Trail on the right. Here your route begins to climb in earnest.
4	Just under 2 miles into the route, reach Horse Cove Gap. If you are enjoying the climb, continue straight (up) to climb to Cat Gap. If you're ready for a reprieve, turn right on Cat Gap Bypass Trail (yellow blaze).

5	Climb 0.4 mile more to get to Cat Gap. Bear right (downhill) to stay on Cat Gap Loop Trail.
6	In another mile you'll see where the bypass trail enters; in yet another mile Butter Gap Trail enters from the left. Stay on the Cat Gap Loop.
7	Just a few tenths of a mile beyond the Butter Gap junction, listen and look for a waterfall down on the creek to the right. A side trail leads steeply down to the falls and another leads less steeply back.
8	Soon you cross a gravel road and then a footbridge. In no time you arrive back at the Fish Hatchery and Wildlife Center.

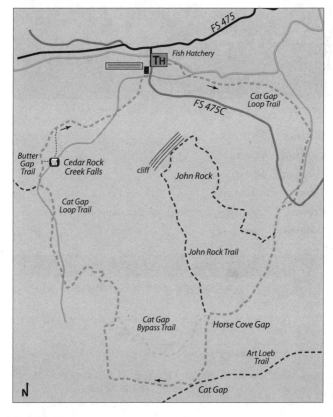

Caney Bottom Loop

Make sure to use the footbridges to cross Cove Creek, not the fords.

Distance	5-mile loop
Difficulty	Moderate
Location	West of Fish Hatchery
Time	3 to 4 hours
Crowds	Light (expect people in group campsite on weekends)
Trailhead	Cove Creek

Route Directions	
1	Walk across the road and around the gate, down the entrance road to Cove Creek Group Camp.
2	At 0.4 mile pass Caney Bottom Loop Trail on the left. You'll come back on this trail. Continue through the campground on the road.
3	Just beyond the first open field you'll pass Baby Sliding Rock Falls on the right.
4	Continue across the second open field and onto the foot trail beyond. Soon you'll intersect with the Caney Bottom Loop Trail (blue blaze).

5	The trail descends steeply for 300 feet, reaching the river level.
6	Within the next mile you'll pass another waterfall and then reach a 4-way trail junction. Turn left here on Cove Creek Trail (yellow blaze).
7	1.7 miles down Cove Creek Trail, look for a sign on the left that reads "Falls". Follow this side trail down a steep hill to view Cove Creek Falls.
8	Cove Creek Trail ends in 0.5 mile. Continue straight on Caney Bottom.
9	Cross a small creek, turn left, continue a short distance, and then turn right to follow the entrance road back to the trailhead.

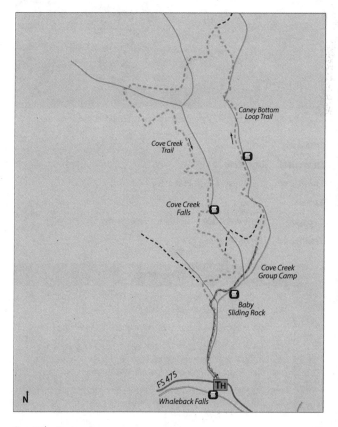

Daniel Ridge Loop

Circle the loop counterclockwise and visit Toms Spring Falls first on the way.

Distance	4-mile loop
Difficulty	Moderate
Location	Just west of Fish Hatchery
Time	3 hours
Crowds	Light weekdays, moderate weekends
Trailhead	Daniel Ridge

Route Directions	
1	Walk out the back of the parking area, around the gate and across the wide bridge on Daniel Ridge Loop Trail (red blaze).
2	Just past the bridge, the trail forks. Bear right on the old gravel road.
3	After 0.5 mile Daniel Ridge Loop trail turns left off the roadway. But first, to view Toms Spring Falls from the bottom, continue on the road another 100 yards. When you're ready, backtrack to the turnoff and head up the trail.
4	Climb for a mile, crossing the creek several times on log bridges, and then cross an old road. This is the same road you were on earlier.

5	Another 0.5 mile brings you to the top of the ridge where an unmarked trail enters from the right. Stay straight and head downhill.
6	A half-mile farther still, reach a junction with Farlow Gap Trail. Turn left down the wooden steps to stay on Daniel Ridge Loop Trail.
7	At the bottom of the steep section, bear left to stay on the trail. There was once a bridge on the right here; now it's just a big hole.
8	A mile beyond the old bridge site turn right, cross the bridge, and you are done.

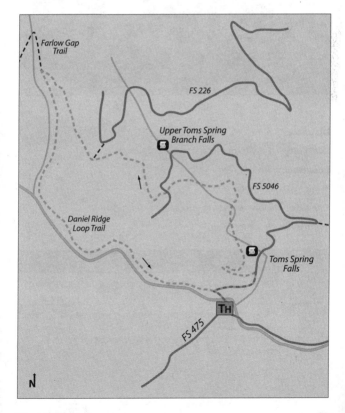

Farlow Gap Trail

FS 226

Upper Toms Spring Branch Falls

FS 5046

Daniel Ridge Loop Trail

Toms Spring Falls

TH

FS 475

N

Twin Falls

Two creeks tumble over the same cliff, 50 yards apart.

Distance	4.1 miles, out and back
Difficulty	Easy to moderate ·
Location	Avery Creek
Time	3 hours
Crowds	Light weekdays, moderate weekends
Trailhead	Buckhorn Gap

Route Directions	
1	From the small parking area, walk directly onto the Buckhorn Gap Trail (orange blaze) and walk gently downhill toward the creek.
2	Reach Avery Creek after 0.9 mile. Bear left on Avery Creek/Buckhorn Gap Trail.
3	After another 0.1 mile, cross the creek on a log footbridge to continue on Buckhorn Gap Trail.

| 4 | Continue on Buckhorn Gap Trail for close to a mile to intersect with the Twin Falls Loop Trail (yellow blaze). Turn left to make the short walk up to the base of the falls. |
| 5 | Explore around the base of both falls as you like, then return to the trailhead the same way you came. |

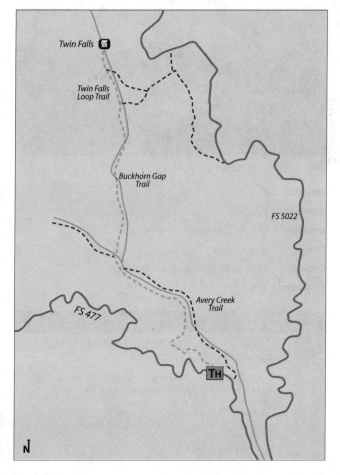

Twin Falls

Twin Falls
Loop Trail

Buckhorn Gap
Trail

FS 5022

FS 477

Avery Creek
Trail

TH

N

Pink Beds Loop

Raised wooden walkways carry you over the bogs and swamps.

Distance	5-mile loop
Difficulty	Easy
Location	Cradle of Forestry
Time	3 to 4 hours
Crowds	Light weekdays, moderate weekends
Trailhead	Pink Beds

	Route Directions
1	From the large parking area, walk east onto Pink Beds Loop Trail (orange blaze). Cross the creek and turn left at the split.
2	After 1.5 miles cross Barnett Branch Trail. If you want to shorten your hike, turn right on this trail and cut across to the other side of the loop.
3	Walk for another 1.2 miles to where the trail makes a T-intersection. Left leads to the Wolf Ford Gauging Station. Turn right here to continue around the loop.

4	Soon you'll begin passing an open bog; then the trail leaves the bogs for a short jaunt over a ridge.
5	Pink Beds Loop converges with Barnett Branch Trail for a short distance and then crosses the bog on a boardwalk. Bear left to continue around the loop.
6	With about a mile to go, cross bogs and beaver ponds on a long wooded walkway. This is a great spot for birding, and you may even spot a beaver.
7	When you close the loop, turn left to walk back to the trailhead parking lot.

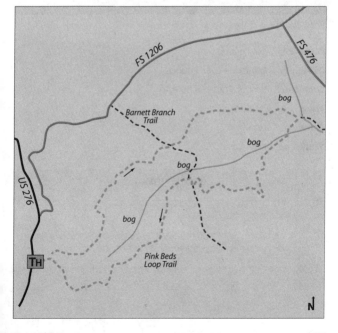

Pilot Cove Loop

Allow time to sit a spell atop Slate Rock. The view is awesome.

Distance	4-mile loop
Difficulty	Moderate to strenuous
Location	East of Cradle of Forestry
Time	3 hours
Crowds	Light
Trailhead	Pilot Cove

Route Directions	
1	From the small trailhead, walk around the gate and up the Pilot Cove/Slate Rock Creek Trail (blue blaze).
2	After 0.2 mile, Pilot Cove Loop Trail exits to the right; you'll come back this way. Continue straight (left), following the blue blazes.
3	A mile-long climb brings you to the top of the ridge. Turn right here on Pilot Cove Loop Trail (yellow blaze).

| 4 | Continue to climb up over two more knobs before reaching Slate Rock. The view is well worth all that climbing. Be very careful here not to get too close to the cliff's edge. Continue around the loop from here. |
| 5 | A steep descent of a little over a mile brings you back down to finish the loop. Turn left and it's an easy walk back to the trailhead. |

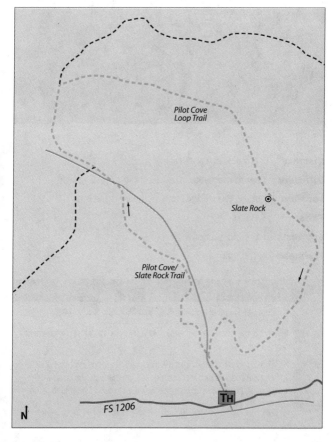

Pilot Cove Loop Trail

Slate Rock

Pilot Cove/ Slate Rock Trail

TH

FS 1206

N

Mount Pisgah

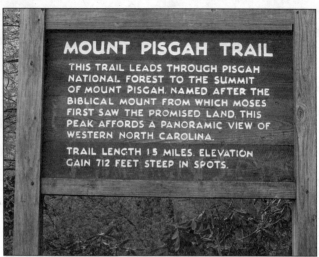

The sign at the trailhead tells you all you need to know.

Distance	2.6 miles, out and back
Difficulty	Easy to moderate
Location	Off the Blue Ridge Parkway near Pisgah Inn
Time	3 hours
Crowds	Light most days
Trailhead	Mt. Pisgah

Route Directions	
1	Walk out the far end of the parking lot onto Mt Pisgah Trail (no blaze).
2	Initially the trail is fairly flat but eventually you'll begin to climb up intermittent stone steps.
3	At 1.3 miles you reach the top of the mountain. There are a number of radio towers here and a short tower/viewing platform that gets you up above the treetops for an expansive, 360 degree view. Once you've had your fill, return the way you came.

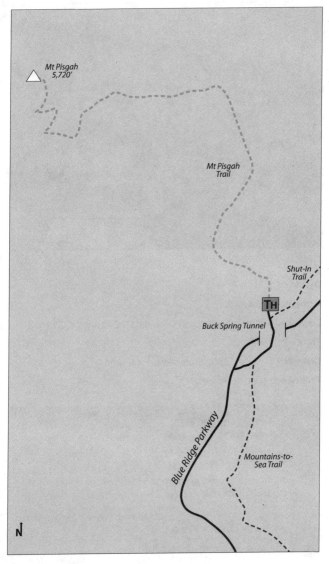

Mt Pisgah
5,720'

Mt Pisgah
Trail

Shut-In
Trail

TH

Buck Spring Tunnel

Blue Ridge Parkway

Mountains-to-
Sea Trail

N

Graveyard Fields

In places, boardwalks lead the way through Graveyard Fields.

Distance	3.3-mile semi-loop
Difficulty	Easy
Location	Blue Ridge Parkway between US 276 and NC 215
Time	2 hours
Crowds	Heavy traffic, especially on weekends
Trailhead	Graveyard Fields

Route Directions	
1	Take Upper Falls Trail (orange blaze) from the west end of the trailhead parking lot. This can be a confusing trail. Follow it down to Yellowstone Prong, cross it, and then head upstream and you should be okay.
2	After about a mile, once you are across Yellowstone Prong, reach a marked trail junction. Bear left to stay close to Yellowstone Prong.
3	In another half-mile, reach Upper Falls. After exploring here, turn around and return to the junction at #2 above.
4	Turn left to connect with Lower Falls Trail.

5	In about a half-mile, Graveyard Ridge Connector Trail exits to the left. Stay on Lower Falls Trail.
6	Soon you will reach a long boardwalk. Continue on.
7	At the end of the boardwalk, bear left down the wooden steps to visit the bottom of Second Falls. Return here and go right, across the top of the water-fall, to return to the trailhead parking lot.

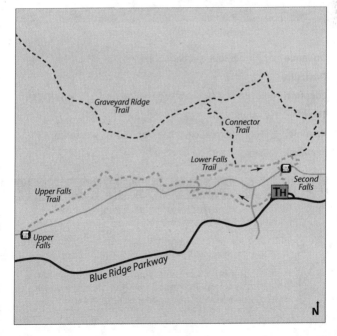

Sam Knob

18

Your destination is always in view as you cross the meadow.

Distance	2.7 miles, out and back
Difficulty	Easy
Location	Just off Blue Ridge Parkway between US 276 and NC 215
Time	2 hours
Crowds	Moderate most days; can be heavy on weekends
Trailhead	Black Balsam

Route Directions	
1	Walk out of the west edge of the parking lot (just to the right of the toilets), around the gate, and onto Sam Knob Trail (no blaze).
2	Descend into a flower-filled meadow on wooden steps and a boardwalk. On the far side, at 0.6 mile, turn right on Sam Knob Summit Trail (blue blaze).
3	The trail winds its way up Sam Knob, tunneling through dense vegetation of flame azaleas, Catawba rhododendron, mountain ash, and yellow birch. Higher up you will break out into open areas with expansive views.

| 4 | Once up top the trail splits, each way going to a separate summit. Both have great views. Turn left to go to the western summit, which you'll reach after climbing 0.6 mile from the meadow. Enjoy the views here, then continue 0.2 mile over to the eastern summit. |
| 5 | Return to the trailhead the way you came up. |

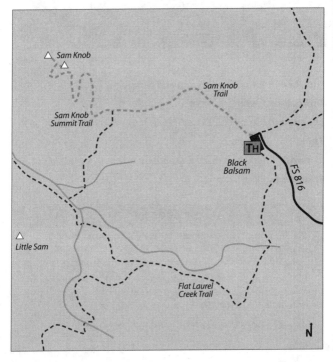

Black Balsam Knob

Wide-open views are common as you climb up to Black Balsam's summit.

Distance	1.4 or 2.6 miles, out and back
Difficulty	Easy to moderate
Location	Just off Blue Ridge Parkway between US 276 and NC 215
Time	2 hours
Crowds	Heavy on many days, especially during fine weather
Trailhead	Black Balsam

Route Directions	
1	The shorter version of this hike begins at the Black Balsam Trailhead. If no parking there, try beginning a half-mile out, along the road on FS 816 where the Art Loeb Trail crosses. You'll see plenty of cars in both places.
2	From Black Balsam Trailhead, walk out the end of FS 816, around the gate, and onto Ivestor Gap Trail (orange blaze). Just beyond the gate, turn right on Art Loeb Spur Trail (no blaze) to climb up the mountain.
3	At 0.4 mile, gain the ridge and turn left on Art Loeb Trail (white blaze).

| 4 | Climb another 0.3 mile to the summit of Black Balsam, being careful not to bypass around it to the left. Return the way you came. |
| 5 | **From the alternate start on FS 816** Follow the Art Loeb Trail the entire route 1.3 miles up to the summit. Return the way you came. |

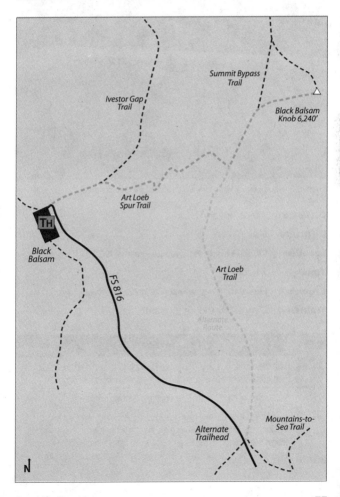

Spot numerous peaks with the aid of the sight device from the summit.

Distance	1 mile, out and back
Difficulty	Easy
Location	On Blue Ridge Parkway just east of NC 215
Time	1 hour
Crowds	Heavy traffic on weekends, moderate weekdays
Trailhead	Devil's Courthouse Overlook

Route Directions	
1	From the overlook, walk up the paved Devil's Courthouse trail that heads north parallel to the Blue Ridge Parkway before turning up the mountain.
2	At 0.3 mile the pavement ends, though the climbing is still steep.
3	In a little less than 0.2 mile more you'll reach the summit, with a viewing area atop the cliff surrounded on three sides by a stone wall. Several sighting devices help you locate distant peaks. Keep an eye out for peregrine falcons, especially early in the morning as they soar high above on the thermals.

4	After you have had your fill of views, return to the parking area the same way you came up.

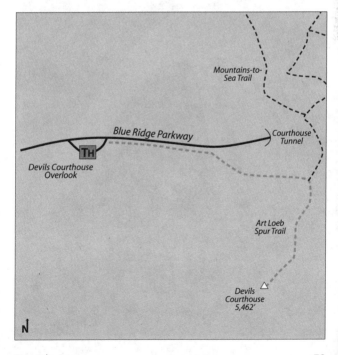

Pisgah Forest

Overnight Hike Routes

Cat Gap via John Rock

This falls on Cedar Rock Creek is just off the trail to Cat Gap.

Distance	5.8-mile loop
Difficulty	Easy
Location	Fish Hatchery
Time	2 days
Crowds	Light weekdays, heavy weekends
Trailhead	Fish Hatchery

Route Directions	
1	Hike past the wildlife center building, go around the gate, and turn right on Cat Gap Loop Trail (orange blaze).
2	At 0.9 mile pass the first of five campsites on this side of the mountain. This one is at the base of a small waterfall.
3	Just 0.1 mile farther along, bear left as Butter Gap Trail exits to the right.
4	When you reach Cat Gap Bypass Trail (yellow blaze) in 1.0 mile more, turn left on it to avoid the steep climb to Cat Gap.

5	At Horse Cove Gap, turn left on John Rock Trail (yellow blaze) to climb up and over John Rock. A steep 0.1-mile climb is just ahead.
6	Pass through a dry campsite and soon you are on top of John Rock. Enjoy the views, but be extremely careful near the edge.
7	A mile more and you'll turn left back onto Cat Gap Loop Trail.
8	In 0.1 mile, reach the first of five campsites on this side of the mountain.
9	Finish your hike along the Davidson River.

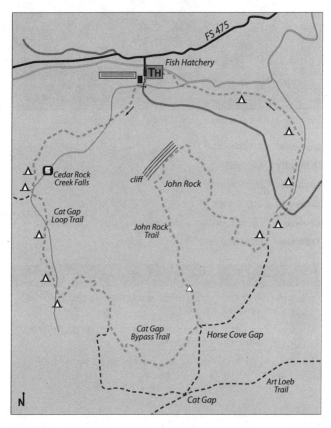

Butter Gap Shelter

You can stay in the shelter at Butter Gap or pitch a tent nearby.

Distance	8.3-mile loop
Difficulty	Moderate
Location	Fish Hatchery
Time	2 or 3 days
Crowds	Light weekdays, moderate weekends
Trailhead	Fish Hatchery

	Route Directions
1	Hike past the wildlife center building, go around the gate, and turn right on Cat Gap Loop Trail (orange blaze).
2	At 0.9 mile pass the first of four campsites before the Butter Gap Shelter. This one is at the base of a small waterfall.
3	Just 0.1 mile farther along, turn right on Butter Gap Trail (blue blaze). You will stay on this trail all the way up to the gap.

4	In 2.6 miles, reach Butter Gap and turn left on Art Loeb Trail (white blaze). It's 0.1 mile farther to the shelter.
5	From the shelter, continue along Art Loeb Trail for 2.4 miles to reach Cat Gap. Here, shift onto Cat Gap Loop Trail (orange blaze).
6	A steep 0.3-mile descent brings you to Horse Cove Gap. Continue down the Cat Gap Loop Trail.
7	Beyond the junction with John Rock Trail, you'll pass four more campsites before you reach the trailhead.
8	Return to the trailhead parking area, finishing up along the Davidson River.

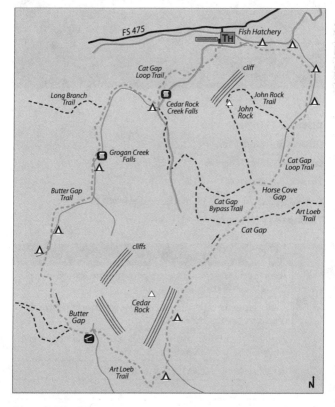

Be sure to take the short detour to view Cove Creek Falls.

Distance	16.8-mile loop
Difficulty	Moderate
Location	Fish Hatchery
Time	3 days
Crowds	Light weekdays, moderate weekends
Trailhead	Fish Hatchery

	Route Directions
1	Hike past the wildlife center building, go around the gate, and turn right on Cat Gap Loop Trail (orange blaze).
2	At 0.9 mile pass the first of five campsites on this side of the mountain. This one is at the base of a small waterfall.
3	Just 0.1 mile farther along, bear left as Butter Gap Trail exits to the right. You'll stay on Cat Gap Loop Trail all the way to Cat Gap.
4	At Cat Gap, turn right on Art Loeb Trail (white blaze).

5	Continue another 2.4 miles to the shelter at Butter Gap, passing two campsites along the way.
6	Stay on Art Loeb Trail to Butter Gap, where you will turn right and descend on Butter Gap Trail (blue blaze).
7	In the next 2.3 miles, pass three campsites and Grogan Creek Falls, then turn left on Long Branch Trail.
8	Continue 0.9 mile on Long Branch Trail to a junction with FS 5095. Turn right down this gated forest road.
9	When you reach FS 475, turn right and make a short descent to Daniel Ridge Trailhead.
10	Walk around the gate, cross the bridge, and bear right toward the falls on Daniel Ridge Loop Trail (red blaze). This part of the trail shares the tread with FS 5046.
11	When the loop trail exits to the left, just before 150-ft Toms Spring Falls, continue on FS 5046 up the hill.
12	Up the grassy road a quarter-mile the road switchbacks to the left. Make a right turn here, off the road, onto an unmarked trail.
13	In just a short distance down this trail, as you near the group camp, turn left on Caney Bottom Loop Trail (blue blaze).
14	Go 0.3 mile and Caney Bottom Loop Trail exits to the right. Stay straight now on Cove Creek Trail (yellow blaze). This trail makes a gradual climb for the next 2.2 miles, passing a side trail to Cove Creek Falls and a couple of small campsites along the way.
15	Just after crossing a small creek, reach a 4-way intersection. Turn left and continue about 100 ft to a large and very nice campsite. To continue the route, bear right here on Caney Bottom Loop Trail.
16	One mile down the trail through dense vegetation and over several log bridges, Caney Bottom Loop Trail exits uphill to the right. Bear left here on an unmarked trail that heads into the fields of Cove Creek Group Camp.
17	When you reach the group camp, walk across the field and onto the roadway that cuts through the campground.
18	Just as you enter the second field you come to in the group camp, look to your left to find Baby Sliding Rock. This is a great spot to take a break and go for a natural water slide.

A tarp makes a nice lightweight alternative to a tent.

19	Continue on out to the entrance for Cove Creek Group Camp, being sure to use the footbridges instead of fording the stream.
20	At the entrance to the group camp, cross over FS 475, bear left a short distance past the small parking lot, and turn right on Davidson River Trail (blue blaze).
21	Davidson River Trail is 1.3 miles long and not so interesting, as it is high above the river. It ends at a gate. Turn right here and walk down the side of paved FS 475.
22	Finish where you began at the Pisgah Fish Hatchery.

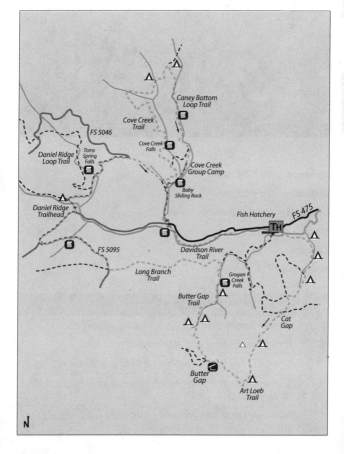

Deep Gap Shelter

Early morning mist hangs in the valleys below Pilot Mountain.

Distance	18.7-mile loop
Difficulty	Very difficult
Location	Fish Hatchery and west
Time	3 days
Crowds	Light
Trailhead	Fish Hatchery

	Route Directions
1	Walk out the entrance to the fish hatchery and turn left on FS 475.
2	After 0.6 mile, turn left on Davidson River Trail (blue blaze).
3	At the end of this trail, turn left and then right into Cove Creek Group Camp.
4	Just before entering the group camp in 0.4 mile, turn left on Caney Bottom Trail (blue blaze).
5	When Caney Bottom Trail turns right across a small creek, continue straight on an unmarked connector trail to FS 5046.

6	Several tenths of a mile later turn left down FS 5046, a grassy road.
7	A quarter-mile farther along, pass Toms Spring Falls on the right, continue down the road, and turn left on Daniel Ridge Loop Trail (red blaze) just before the big bridge over the upper Davidson River.
8	Daniel Ridge Loop Trail gently climbs beside the river for a mile or so where you'll pass some campsites down the steep hill to your left. If you choose one of these for your first night out you can start the climbing fresh. From here the trail turns steeply up the hill for another half-mile to intersect with Farlow Gap Trail.
9	Turn left on Farlow Gap Trail (blue blaze) and continue to climb intermittently.
10	After 2.3 miles cross the top of Shuck Ridge Creek Falls. Soon after, the trail turns very steeply up the mountain to make its final climb to Farlow Gap.
11	At Farlow Gap turn left on Art Loeb Trail (white blaze) to climb over Sassafras Knob. Alternatively, take the old woods road to bypass this climb—it's the same distance no matter which way you go.
12	From Farlow Gap it's about 1.5 miles to Deep Gap Shelter. Theres a campsite just down the hill. Be aware that there are no campsites with water for the next 6 miles beyond the shelter.
13	Cross over the top of Pilot Mountain before making a 2-mile descent to Gloucester Gap.
14	At Gloucester Gap, cross FS 475 to stay on Art Loeb Trail.
15	Continue 0.6 mile and cross FS 471 to stay on Art Loeb Trail.
16	Pass a few dry campsites in the next stretch. Go another 2.6 miles and turn left on Butter Gap Trail (orange blaze). If you plan to use Butter Gap Shelter, stay on Art Loeb Trail for 0.1 mile.
17	Continuing 0.7 mile down Butter Gap Trail, you'll come to the first of two nice campsites on Grogan Creek.
18	Beyond the campsites you'll pass Grogan Creek Falls on the right and then intersect with Long Branch Trail. Stay straight here on Butter Gap Trail and continue down to a junction with Cat Gap Loop Trail in another half-mile.
19	Turn left on Cat Gap Loop Trail (orange blaze), pass a campsite by a small waterfall, and continue on down the trail.
20	Cat Gap Loop Trail crosses a forest road and then a footbridge, and then finally ends just behind the wildlife center.
21	Turn left on the gated road and go around the gate to finish where you began.

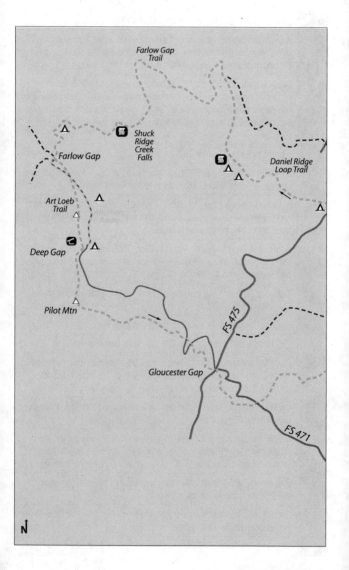

Farlow Gap
Trail

Shuck
Ridge
Creek
Falls

Farlow Gap

Daniel Ridge
Loop Trail

Art Loeb
Trail

alternate
route

Deep Gap

Pilot Mtn

FS 475

Gloucester Gap

FS 471

N

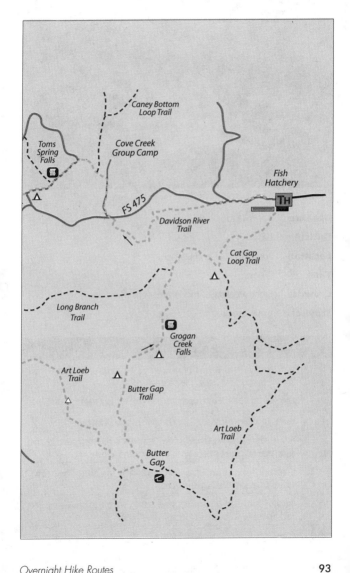

Caney Bottom
Loop Trail

Toms
Spring
Falls

Cove Creek
Group Camp

Fish
Hatchery

FS 475

Davidson River
Trail

Cat Gap
Loop Trail

Long Branch
Trail

Grogan
Creek
Falls

Art Loeb
Trail

Butter Gap
Trail

Art Loeb
Trail

Butter
Gap

Caney Bottom

Baby Sliding Rock is located on Cove Creek.

Distance	4.9-mile loop
Difficulty	Easy
Location	Just west of Fish Hatchery
Time	2 days
Crowds	Light weekdays, moderate weekends
Trailhead	Cove Creek

Route Directions	
1	Walk across the road, around the gate, and up the group camp entrance road into the campground proper. There are two big fields.
3	Continue across the second open field and onto the foot trail beyond.
4	Bear right to merge with the Caney Bottom Loop Trail (blue blaze).
5	At 2.0 miles reach a junction with Cove Creek Trail. For the best campsite, turn right here and go just short ways to the big shady campsite.
6	Continuing the loop, turn left on Cove Creek Trail (yellow blaze). There are a couple of small campsites farther along.
7	In 1.7 miles from the big campsite, reach a short side trail to view Cove Creek Falls. Tip: Leave your packs at the top.
8	Cove Creek Trail ends in about 0.5 mile. Continue straight on Caney Bottom.

| 9 | Go another 0.3 mile, cross a tiny creek, and turn left. |
| 10 | In just a short distance turn right, back onto the entrance road, to head back to the trailhead parking lot. |

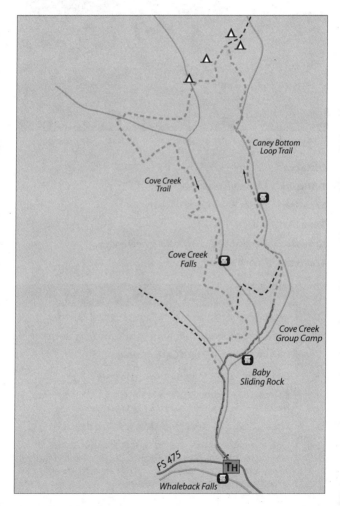

Clawhammer Mountain

Wooden signs replace the usual carsonite wands at Club Gap.

Distance	13.3-mile loop
Difficulty	Moderate to difficult
Location	Circles Avery Creek Watershed
Time	2 days
Crowds	Light weekdays, moderate weekends
Trailhead	Coontree Picnic Area

Route Directions	
1	Walk across the highway and onto the Coontree Loop Trail (blue blaze).
2	After 0.2 mile the trail splits. Take the left fork to begin your first steep climb.
3	In 1.6 miles turn left on Bennett Gap Trail (red blaze).
4	Gradually climb 0.7 mile to reach a fantastic view spot.
5	It's another 0.7 mile to cross FS 477 at Bennett Gap. Cross onto Buckwheat Knob Trail (yellow blaze). Two short but steep climbs follow.
6	Reach Club Gap in 1.5 miles. Begin Black Mountain Trail (white blaze).
7	Climb again, over Rich Mountain and down to Buckhorn Gap shelter and campsite. This is the only good camping area on this loop. The shelter will hold a small group (6-8). Campsites are near the shelter and also on the other side of the trail. Look for the spring behind the shelter.

8	Cross FS 5048 at Buckhorn Gap, just down from the shelter, to stay on Black Mountain Trail. Now you'll climb over Clawhammer and Black Mountain.
9	In 1.2 miles top out for more great views.
10	Hike downhill a mile or so to Pressley Gap. Turn right here on FS 5098, go 0.2 mile, and look closely for a set of wooden steps going down on the left. Follow the steps down; this is Pressley Cove Trail (orange blaze).
11	Descend 1.2 miles through the cove to reach FS 477. Turn left here, cross the bridge over the creek, and immediately turn right on Bennett Gap Trail.
12	Climb back up Bennett Gap Trail for just over a mile and turn left on Coontree Loop Trail to go steeply back down.
13	Reach the other end of Coontree Loop. Turn left to finish the hike.

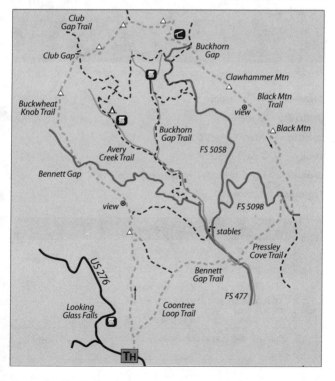

Buckhorn Gap Shelter

Don't miss the mountain spring located behind Buckhorn Gap shelter.

Distance	9.4-mile loop
Difficulty	Moderate
Location	Avery Creek Watershed
Time	2 days
Crowds	Light weekdays, moderate weekends
Trailhead	Buckhorn Gap

Route Directions	
1	Walk down Buckhorn Gap Trail (orange blaze).
2	Just before the creek bear left on Avery Creek/Buckhorn Gap Trail.
3	At the 1.0-mile mark, turn left on Avery Creek Trail (blue blaze). Don't cross the footbridge which is the continuation of Buckhorn Gap Trail.
4	After an 0.8-mile ascent you'll pass a large campsite.
5	Continue 2 miles more to Club Gap to turn right on Black Mountain Trail (white blaze).

6	Climb up and over Rich Mountain to reach Buckhorn Gap Shelter in another couple of miles.
7	From the shelter, head downhill a short distance to Buckhorn Gap. Cross the road here on Black Mountain Trail and as soon as you enter the woods, turn right on.Buckhorn Gap Trail (orange blaze).
8	In 0.4 mile, turn left on FS 5058.
9	Continue a half-mile and turn right, back onto Buckhorn Gap Trail.
10	At the bottom of the hill, turn right to stay on Buckhorn Gap Trail.
11	Pass the turnoff to view Twin Falls. Continue on Buckhorn Gap Trail all the way back to the trailhead where you began.

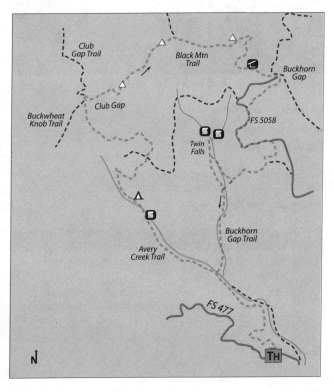

Pink Beds Loop Trail is fairly level, but the climb to Buckhorn Gap is not.

Distance	10.6-mile loop
Difficulty	Moderate (2-day) or easy (3-day)
Location	Pink Beds area
Time	2 or 3 days
Crowds	Light weekdays, moderate weekends
Trailhead	Pink Beds

Route Directions	
1	Walk around the gate and onto the Pink Beds Loop Trail (orange blaze). When it splits, take the right fork.
2	In the first 1.5 miles you'll cross a long boardwalk over bog and swamp. Where Barnett Branch Trail heads off to the left over another boardwalk, bear right to stay on the Pink Beds Loop. 1
3	In another 1.2 miles reach a fine campsite. Just beyond it, turn right on Pink Beds Extension Trail.

4	Continue 0.6 mile to reach a roadside campsite, a gauging station, and the end of FS 476. Go around the gate here onto South Mills River Trail (white blaze).
5	The trail follows the river, then crosses a bridge and heads uphill. At 2.0 miles from the gauging station, bear right onto Buckhorn Gap Trail (orange blaze).
6	Continue 0.8 mile farther to reach Buckhorn Gap. Turn right here and head up the wooden steps on Black Mountain Trail (white blaze). Buckhorn Gap shelter and campsite is just up the trail.
7	From the shelter, continue another mile up the mountain to turn right on Barnett Branch Trail (blue blaze).
8	Hike down the mountain 2.0 miles and turn left, back onto Pink Beds Loop Trail. Continue another 1.5 miles back to the trailhead.

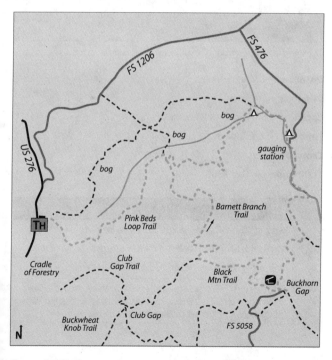

Crossing the Big East Fork of the Pigeon River can be tricky.

Distance	12.7-mile loop
Difficulty	Strenuous
Location	Shining Rock Wilderness
Time	2 or 3 days
Crowds	Light
Trailhead	Big East Fork

Route Directions	
1	Walk past the info kiosk and up Shining Creek Trail (no blaze).
2	After 0.3 mile turn right, away from the river, and head up the mountain.
3	After another 0.4 mile, stay left as Old Butt Knob Trail exits right.
4	Climb forever (4.0 miles total from river), crossing creeks and streams to finally top out on Art Loeb Trail at Shining Rock Gap. There are campsites here, both to the left and right. Turn left on Art Loeb Trail to continue.

5	Partway around Grassy Cove Top, turn left on an unmarked trail to connect with Grassy Cove Trail (no blaze).
6	Head down the mountain for 3.0 miles to cross the Big East Fork at a campsite. On the far side, turn left on Big East Fork Trail (no blaze).
7	Follow along the Big East Fork for the next 3.7 miles to finish.

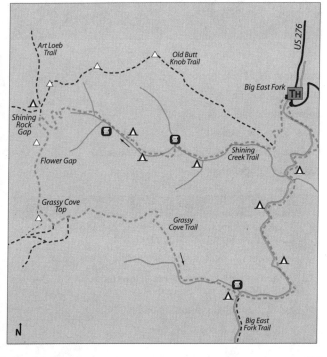

Graveyard Ridge

You'll cross over 6,056-ft. Tennent Mountain on this route.

Distance	13.3-mile loop
Difficulty	Strenuous
Location	Shining Rock Wilderness
Time	2 or 3 days
Crowds	Light weekdays, moderate weekends
Trailhead	Black Balsam

	Route Directions
1	Walk back up the road you drove in on and turn left, then bear right on the Mountains-to-Sea Trail (MST; white dot blaze).
2	In another 1.5 miles turn right on Graveyard Ridge Trail (orange blaze).
3	Circle Graveyard Ridge and then turn right to get back on the MST. Stick to the MST as you travel through Graveyard Fields and past Second Falls.
4	A long downhill brings you to Skinny Dip Falls.

5	Just before reaching the Blue Ridge Parkway, turn left to stay on the MST. A short distance beyond, turn left on Bridges Camp Gap Trail (no blaze), which eventually becomes Big East Fork Trail..
6	Once you reach the river, continue for another 0.7 mile to where there are two campsites, one on each side. Turn left and ford the river here to continue on Grassy Cove Trail (no blaze).
7	After a 3.2-mile climb, turn right on Graveyard Ridge Trail (no blaze). You can see Ivestor Gap just ahead of you.
8	At Ivestor Gap turn left on Art Loeb Trail. Follow it through the next gap and up and over Tennent Mountain, then Black Balsam Knob.
9	Once over Black Balsam Knob, turn right on Art Loeb Spur to walk back down to the trailhead.

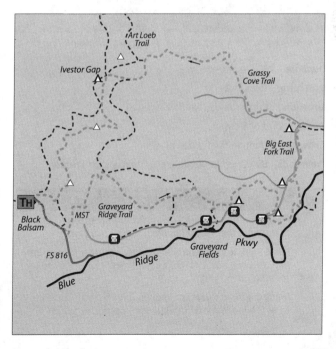

Art Loeb Trail

An exposed spot, but what a place for star gazing at Ivestor Gap!

Distance	30.1 miles, one way
Difficulty	Strenuous
Location	Crosses Pisgah North to South
Time	4 or 5 days
Crowds	Light on most sections
Trailheads	BSA Camp Daniel Boone & Pisgah Ranger Station

Route Directions	
	You can hike the Art Loeb Trail in either direction. These directions are north to south, finishing at the ranger station. You will need to run a shuttle.
1	**Daniel Boone to Ivestor Gap** Good campsites at Deep Gap (3.8 mile), Crawford Creek Gap (6 mile), Shining Rock Gap (7.1 mile), Flower Gap (7.8 mile), and Ivestor Gap (8.9 mile).
2	**Ivestor Gap to Deep Gap** Good campsites at FS 816 crossing (3.2 mile), Farlow Gap (6.2 mile), and Deep Gap shelter (7.3 mile).

Pisgah's premier long-distance trail

| 3 | **Deep Gap shelter to Butter Gap Shelter** No good campsites in between due to lack of water. Stay at or adjacent to shelters. |
| 4 | **Butter Gap shelter to US 276 at Ranger Station** No good campsites in between due to lack of water. |

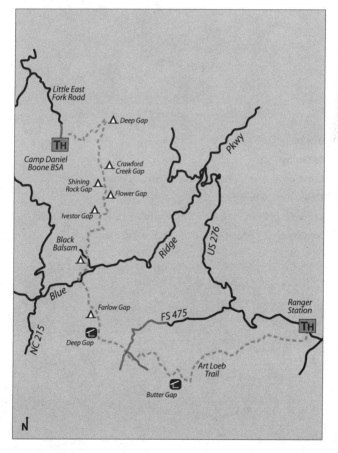

Check your map and follow the white dot blaze to stay on the MST.

Distance	39.7 miles, one way
Difficulty	Strenuous
Location	Crosses Pisgah west to east
Time	4 to 5 days
Crowds	Light most places; can be heavy near Graveyard Fields
Trailheads	Bearpen Gap & BRP Access at NC Arboretum

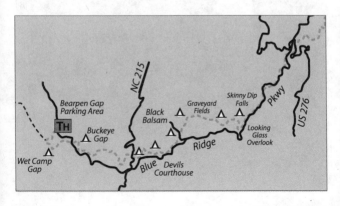

Route Directions

You can hike the MST in either direction. These directions are west to east, finishing adjacent to the NC Arboretum in Asheville. You will need to run a shuttle. **Note** Camping is not permitted on Blue Ridge Parkway lands.

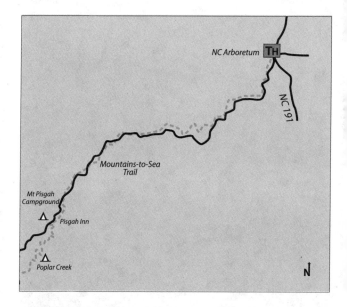

1	**Bearpen Gap to Devil's Courthouse** Good campsites at Wet Camp Gap (1.4 miles), Buckeye Gap Trail junction (5.2 miles), either side of NC 215, (8.6 miles) and the trail junction to the Devil's Courthouse (11.4 miles).
2	**Devil's Courthouse to Looking Glass Overlook on the Blue Ridge Parkway** Good campsites at crossing of FS 816 (2.1miles), Graveyard Fields (6.0 miles), and Skinny Dip Falls (7.3 miles).
3	**Looking Glass Overlook to Mt. Pisgah Campground** Good Campsites at east of Poplar Creek (6.5 miles) and Mt. Pisgah Campground (11.2 miles)
4	**Mt. Pisgah Campground to NC Arboretum** No good campsites on this section due to lack of water on sections not on Blue Ridge Parkway lands.

HIKING & MOUNTAIN BIKING PISGAH FOREST

Pisgah Forest

Mountain Bike Routes

Hardtimes Loop

Trailheads are well marked in Bent Creek.

Distance	6-mile loop
Difficulty	Easy
Location	Bent Creek
Time	1 to 2 hours
Crowds	Moderate weekdays, heavy weekends
Trailhead	Hardtimes

Route Directions	
1	Ride out the back end of the parking lot and around the gate.
2	At 0.2 mile turn right, and after a short distance turn left across the bridge onto Hardtimes Road.
3	The road gradually climbs the hill for the next couple of miles. Roads will exit to either side; just stay on Hardtimes Road, eventually paralleling the Blue Ridge Parkway.
4	Pass through the fence into the NC Arboretum.
5	Check your speed as you descend into the Arboretum; you will encounter walkers coming up. After another mile, turn left just before a parking area to parallel the entrance road.

6	A little bit farther on turn left on Old Bent Creek Road, which follows the creek.
7	Ride a little more than a mile through the Arboretum proper before finally passing through another fenced area. From here it is about a mile back to the trailhead.

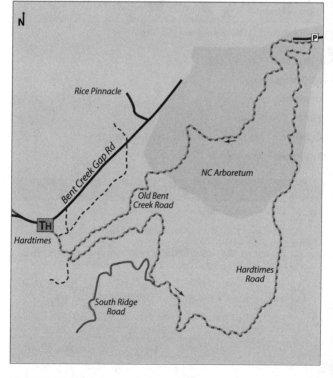

Rice Pinnacle

The single track is pretty easy on Deer Lake Lodge Trail.

Distance	4.8-mile loop
Difficulty	Easy
Location	Bent Creek
Time	1+ hour
Crowds	Moderate weekdays, heavy weekends
Trailhead	Rice Pinnacle

	Route Directions
1	Ride out of the parking area and up Rice Pinnacle Road (FS 491).
2	After 1.2 miles turn left on Ledford Branch Road (FS 479E).
3	Turn right on Hilltop Trail at 1.2 miles to begin fun single track. Several trails exit off this road on the left and on the right. Just stay on the road.
4	Just under 1.5 miles on this road brings you to Ledford Gap. There are a few picnic tables here. Bear left to stay on FS 479E as FS 479F exits right.
5	In 0.8 mile reach Ledford Branch trailhead parking. Head straight for the toilet and then turn left just before it onto Deer Lake Lodge Trail (orange blaze).
6	Go 0.3 mile and bear left under the powerlines, still on Deer Lake Lodge Trail.

| 7 | Turn right at the bottom of the whoop-te-do hill to remain on Deer Lake Lodge Trail. |
| 8 | From here it's just 0.3 mile back to the trailhead where you began. |

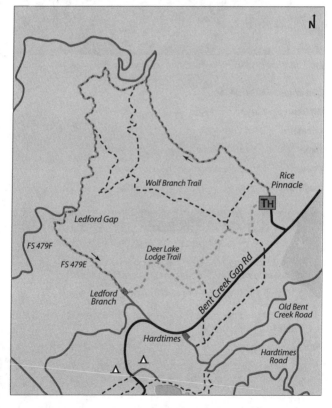

Deerfield–Explorer–Pine Tree

You'll spin out past Lake Powhatan on your way to the loops.

Distance   6.8-mile loop

Difficulty   Easy to moderate

Location   Bent Creek

Time   1.5 to 3 hours

Crowds   Moderate weekdays, heavy weekends

Trailhead   Hardtimes

	Route Directions
1	Ride out of the back of the parking lot, around the gate, and down the road.
2	At 0.2 mile turn right along the creek. Go a short ways and turn left across the bridge, then go immediately right on Homestead Trail (orange blaze).
3	After 0.4 mile turn left at the split on Small Creek Trail (red blaze).
4	Up the hill 0.3 mile, go up the wooden steps and onto Deerfield Loop Trail (yellow blaze).
5	A half-mile farther along, turn left on Pine Tree Loop Trail (blue blaze).
6	Follow Pine Tree for a mile, then turn left on the connector trail which leads to Explorer Loop Trail (yellow blaze), where you'll turn left.

7	Circle Explorer back to this same spot, then continue around Pine Tree Loop.
8	When you reach the paved campground road turn left, cross the creek ,and then turn right on the fishermen's access road to ride beside Lake Powhatan.
9	At the spillway, ride over the hump and down alongside Bent Creek. Soon you'll turn left to head back to the trailhead.

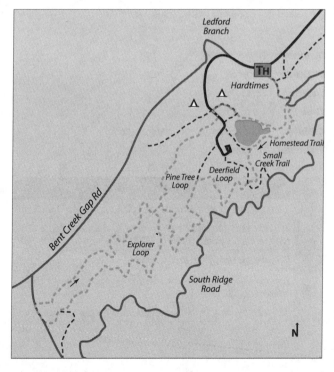

South Ridge

The second half of the ride follows Lower Sidehill Trail.

Distance	10.9-mile loop
Difficulty	Moderate
Location	Bent Creek
Time	1.5 to 3 hours
Crowds	Light weekdays, moderate weekends
Trailhead	Hardtimes

Route Directions	
1	Ride out of the back of the parking lot, around the gate and down the road.
2	At 0.2 mile turn right along the creek. Go a short ways, turn left across the bridge, and ride up Hardtimes Road.
3	In another mile turn right on South Ridge Road (FS 479M).
4	Follow South Ridge Road for 5.5 miles to its end. Turn left on Bent Creek Gap Road and climb the hill.
5	After a 0.1-mile climb, turn right onto Lower Sidehill Trail (orange blaze).

6	A short distance beyond where Lower Sidehill Connector Trail enters from the right, turn right and follow FS 479G briefly before turning left off the road to remain on Lower Sidehill Trail.
7	Continue on Lower Sidehill Trail until you meet FS 479F. Turn right and ride down and across Bent Creek Gap Road onto Campground Connector Trail (blue blaze).
8	Once in the campground, circle Lake Powhatan on the left. Continue past the fishing access pier, over the hump by the spillway, and down along Bent Creek.
9	Soon you will turn left to follow the road back to the trailhead.

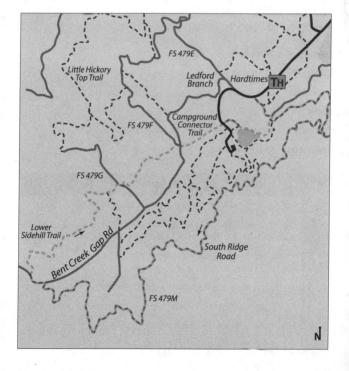

From Ingles Field Gap, the trail descends over small, fun whoops.

Distance	7.9-mile loop
Difficulty	Moderate
Location	Bent Creek
Time	1.5 to 2.5 hours
Crowds	Moderate weekdays, heavy weekends
Trailhead	Rice Pinnacle

	Route Directions
1	Ride out of the parking area and up Rice Pinnacle Road (FS 491).
2	Pass the turn onto Ledford Branch Road at 1.3 miles and continue another 0.1 mile to continue straight onto North Boundary Road (FS 485).
3	As you climb over Wolf Knob, the road goes from double track to single track. Another 2.5 miles brings you to Ingles Field Gap.
4	At the gap, make a near-180-degree turn onto Ingles Field Gap Trail (blue blaze).
5	Go 0.7 mile down the mountain and turn right on Ingles Field Gap Connector.
6	In 0.3 mile you'll reach FS 479F. Turn left and continue down.
7	A quick 0.8 mile later you are at Ledford Gap. Turn left on FS 479E.

8	Go 0.6 mile and turn right on Wolf Branch Trail (yellow blaze).
9	Follow the entire length of Wolf Branch Trail for 1.4 miles. Turn left and follow Deer Lake Lodge Trail (orange blaze) another 0.4 mile to finish where you began.

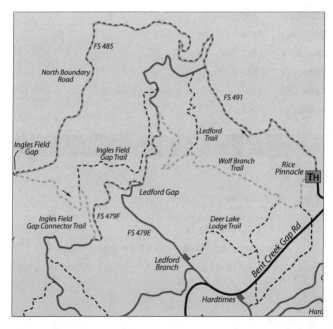

Little Hickory

Little Hickory Top and Sidehill Trails combine for a super-fun downhill.

Distance	7.7-mile loop
Difficulty	Moderate to strenuous
Location	Bent Creek
Time	1.5 to 2.5 hours
Crowds	Moderate weekdays, heavy weekends
Trailhead	Hardtimes

	Route Directions
1	Ride on the road to the Ledford Branch trailhead, around the gate, and up FS 479E.
2	At Ledford Gap turn left on FS 479F.
3	Gradually climb 0.8 mile to turn right on Ingles Field Gap Connector Trail where you'll begin to climb in earnest.
4	After 0.3 mile turn left on Ingles Field Gap Trail (blue blaze). Keep climbing.
5	Another 0.7 mile brings you to the gap. Turn left here on Little Hickory Top Trail (yellow blaze) to begin the descent.
6	Spin down the hill for 1.3 miles and turn right on Sidehill Trail (yellow blaze).

7	In 0.9 mile continue straight onto FS 479G and keep descending.
8	After another 0.6 mile, turn left on Lower Sidehill Trail (orange blaze).
9	Continue to follow Lower Sidehill Trail until you meet FS 479F. Turn right and ride down and across Bent Creek Gap Road onto Campground Connector Trail (blue blaze).
10	Once in the campground, circle Lake Powhatan on the left, past the fishing access pier, over the hump by the spillway, and down along Bent Creek.
11	Turn left to follow the road back to the trailhead.

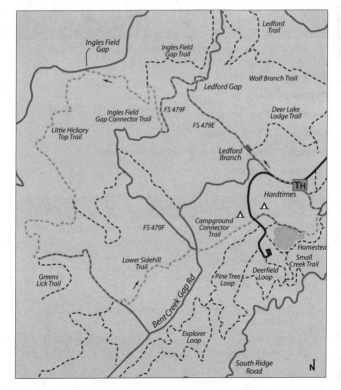

Green's Lick

On Green's Lick, those banked turns come up fast.

Distance	8.8-mile loop
Difficulty	Strenuous
Location	Bent Creek
Time	1.5 to 2.5 hours
Crowds	Moderate weekdays, heavy weekends
Trailhead	Hardtimes

Route Directions	
1	Ride on the road to the Ledford Branch trailhead and then around the gate and up FS 479E.
2	At Ledford Gap, turn left on FS 479F.
3	Climb gradually for 0.8 miles and turn right on Ingles Field Gap Connector Trail.
4	After a steeper 0.3 mile uphill, turn left on Ingles Field Gap Trail (blue blaze). Keep climbing.
5	Another 0.7 mile brings you to the gap. Go straight across onto North Boundary Road (it's a trail here), following signs for Green's Lick Trail.

6	Climb another 1.2 miles and turn left down Green's Lick Trail (red blaze). Get ready for lots of big dirt humps and banked-wall turns.
7	In 2.1 miles turn right onto FS 479G and keep descending.
8	After 0.6 mile turn left on Lower Sidehill Trail (orange blaze).
9	Continue to follow Lower Sidehill Trail until you meet FS 479F. Turn right and ride down and across Bent Creek Gap Road onto Campground Connector Trail (blue blaze).
10	Once in the campground, circle Lake Powhatan on the left. Continue past the fishing access pier, over the hump by the spillway, and down along Bent Creek.
11	Turn left to follow the road back to the trailhead.

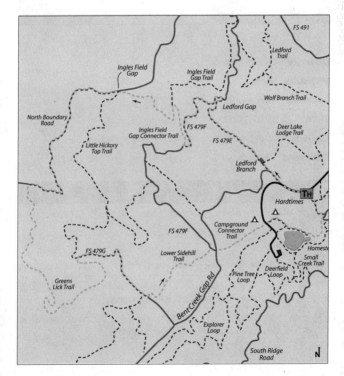

Fletcher Creek

The shallow crossing at Fletcher Creek is a blast.

Distance	9.1-mile loop
Difficulty	Easy
Location	Trace Ridge
Time	1 to 2 hours
Crowds	Light weekdays, moderate weekends
Trailhead	Trace Ridge

Route Directions	
1	Ride out of the parking area around the upper gate onto FS 5097, also known as Never-Ending Road.
2	Spencer Gap Trail crosses the road at 4.6 miles.
3	Continue for another mile and turn left on Fletcher Creek Trail (blue blaze).
4	Ride on this trail for 1.2 miles to cross Fletcher Creek. On the other side, bear right and remain on Fletcher Creek Trail to climb up and over a hill.
5	From the creek crossing 1.1 miles, turn left on FS 142. From here it's another 1.2 miles of gradual climbing back to the trailhead.

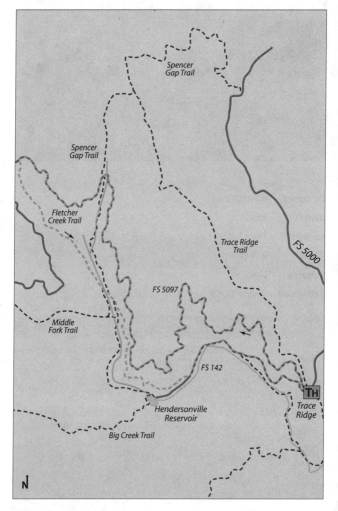

Spencer
Gap Trail

Spencer
Gap Trail

Fletcher
Creek Trail

Trace Ridge
Trail

FS 5000

FS 5097

Middle
Fork Trail

FS 142

TH
Trace
Ridge

Hendersonville
Reservoir

Big Creek Trail

N

Bear Branch

Ferns line Bear Branch Trail.

Distance	4.7-mile loop
Difficulty	Easy
Location	Trace Ridge
Time	1 hour
Crowds	Light
Trailhead	Trace Ridge

	Route Directions
1	Ride out lower Trace Ridge Trail (orange blaze), which is located to the left of the info kiosk at the back of the parking lot.
2	Go downhill for 0.4 mile and make a hard left on Wash Creek Trail (yellow blaze).
3	In another 0.9 mile, the trail ends at FS 142. Turn right to ride down it and cross FS 5000 to the horse camp. Turn left and then right onto Bear Branch Trail (blue blaze).
4	The trail travels for 0.5 mile around the horse camp. At the split, turn left.
5	Go 0.1 mile up the short hill onto a forest road and take a left.
6	Continue 0.2 mile to turn right on FS 5001, Senniard Mountain Road.

7	Ride gradually uphill for 0.8 mile and turn right, back onto Wash Creek Trail.
8	Follow this trail back to the horse camp, cross onto FS 142 and continue back to the trailhead.

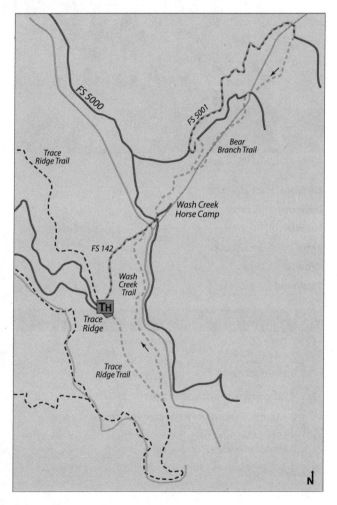

Spencer Gap

Stop for a rest at Hendersonville Reservoir.

Distance	8.1-mile loop
Difficulty	Moderate
Location	Trace Ridge
Time	1 to 2 hours
Crowds	Light
Trailhead	Trace Ridge

Route Directions	
1	Ride out of the parking area around the upper gate onto FS 5097 (a.k.a. Never-Ending Road).
2	At 4.6 miles, turn left on Spencer Gap Trail (orange blaze).
3	Ride beside and through the creek for 0.9 mile to cross Fletcher Creek Trail.
4	Cross the creek again; soon Middle Branch Trail enters from the right.
5	Make one last creek crossing, pass the turnoff for Big Creek Trail, and reach Hendersonville Reservoir. Continue onto FS 142.
6	From the reservoir it's 1.6 miles of gentle climbing back to the trailhead.

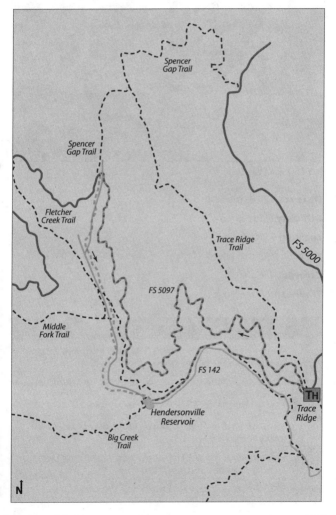

Spencer
Gap Trail

Spencer
Gap Trail

Fletcher
Creek Trail

Trace Ridge
Trail

FS 5000

FS 5097

Middle
Fork Trail

FS 142

Hendersonville
Reservoir

TH
Trace
Ridge

Big Creek
Trail

N

Trace Ridge

Lots of great rides begin at the Trace Ridge Trailhead.

Distance	9.8-mile loop
Difficulty	Strenuous
Location	Trace Ridge
Time	2 to 3 hours
Crowds	Light
Trailhead	Trace Ridge

Route Directions	
1	Ride up Trace Ridge Trail (orange blaze). It starts just to the right of the upper gated road (FS 5097) and climbs steeply right off the bat.
2	After 2.0 miles from the start, turn left on Spencer Gap Trail (yellow blaze).
3	In 0.8 mile turn right on FS 5097 (a.k.a. Never-Ending Road).
4	Stay on the road for 3.3 miles before finally turning left on Middle Fork Trail (orange blaze).
5	Ride down Middle Fork for 1.4 miles, turn left and then right onto Fletcher Creek Trail (blue blaze), then cross Fletcher Creek.
6	Follow Fletcher Creek Trail up and over the ridge for another 1.2 miles.

7 | Turn left on FS 142 and ride back up the gentle hill to the trailhead.

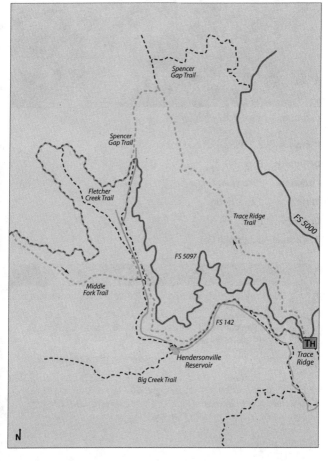

South Mills River

It's a bouncy ride across each bridge.

Distance	7.2 miles, out and back
Difficulty	Easy
Location	Turkeypen Gap
Time	1 to 2 hours
Crowds	Light
Trailhead	Turkeypen Gap

Route Directions	
1	Ride out of the end of the parking lot, around the gate, and onto the road just to the right of the info kiosk.
2	It's 0.8 mile down the hill. At the bottom, turn left on South Mills River Trail (white blaze). The first bridge is just ahead.
3	From here it's 1.6 miles to the second bridge. Along the way, two trails enter from the right.
4	Cross the third and last bridge in another 0.8 mile. Just up ahead is the historic Cantrell Creek Lodge site. All that's left is the chimney; the rest of the lodge stands today at the Cradle of Forestry.

5   This makes a good destination and turn-around spot; the trail gets significantly more difficult ahead with numerous wet river crossings. Return to the trailhead the same way you came.

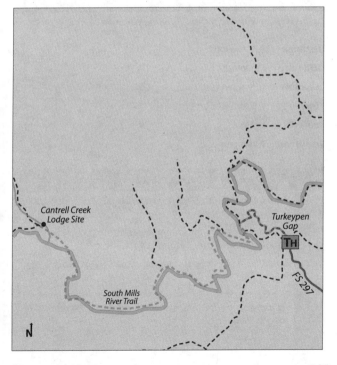

Riverside

You'll get good at river crossings; there are plenty on this ride.

Distance	7.8-mile loop
Difficulty	Moderate
Location	Turkeypen Gap
Time	1.5 to 2.5 hours
Crowds	Light
Trailhead	Turkeypen Gap

Route Directions	
1	Ride out of the end of the parking lot, around the gate, and onto the road just to the right of the info kiosk.
2	It's 0.8 mile to the bottom of the hill where you'll turn right on Bradley Creek Trail (orange blaze). The first river crossing is half a mile ahead.
3	Beyond the first river crossing 0.2 mile, turn left up the hill on Bradley Creek Trail.
4	At Pea Gap, Squirrel Gap Trail enters from the left. Continue down the hill and just after crossing a small creek, turn right on Vineyard Gap Trail (yellow blaze) and cross Bradley Creek.

| 5 | After another mile turn right on Riverside Trail (blue blaze). Cross Bradley Creek again and ride up beside the South Mills River. |
| 6 | Cross the river four times in the next 2.1 miles to finally turn left, back onto Bradley Creek Trail, and finish the ride they way you started. |

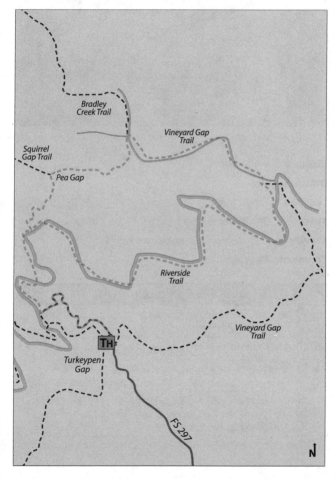

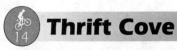

Thrift Cove

Banked turns and wooden bridges are the norm on this loop.

Distance	4-mile loop
Difficulty	Easy
Location	Ranger Station
Time	30 minutes to 1 hour
Crowds	Light weekdays, moderate weekends
Trailhead	Black Mountain

	Route Directions
1	Ride out the back end of the parking area and around the gate up Black Mountain Trail (white blaze).
2	At 0.2 mile, turn right on Thrift Cove Trail (red blaze). It's more like a road here.
3	Up the road 0.1 mile, a connector to Sycamore Cove Trail exits to the right. Just beyond this, Grassy Road Trail also exits to the right. Stay on Thrift Cove.
4	The road/trail very gradually climbs through the cove for the next 2 miles or so before looping back down again. At this point Thrift Cove Trail ends; continue on Black Mountain Trail. Let the fun begin!
5	You'll fly downhill for the next 1.5 miles, all the way back to the trailhead.

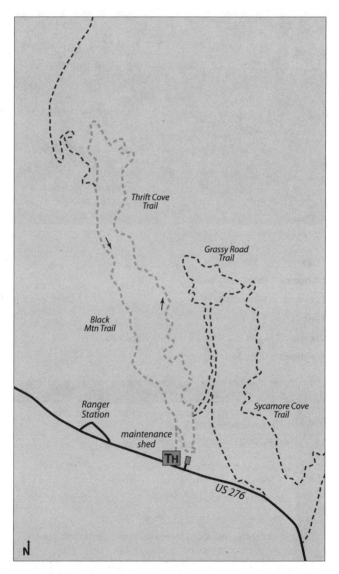

Thrift Cove Trail

Grassy Road Trail

Black Mtn Trail

Sycamore Cove Trail

Ranger Station

maintenance shed

TH

US 276

N

Sycamore Cove

Carsonite wand-style signs direct you through Pisgah.

Distance	4.5-mile loop
Difficulty	Easy to moderate
Location	Ranger Station
Time	1 to 1.5 hours
Crowds	Light weekdays, moderate weekends
Trailhead	Black Mountain

	Route Directions
1	Ride out the back end of the parking area and around the gate up Black Mountain Trail (white blaze).
2	At 0.2 mile, turn right on Thrift Cove Trail (red blaze). It's more like a road here.
3	Up the road 0.1 mile, a connector to Sycamore Cove Trail exits to the right. Just beyond this, turn right on Grassy Road Trail (orange blaze).
4	After 1.0 mile more, turn left on Sycamore Cove Trail (blue blaze).
5	Follow Sycamore Cove Trail for 1.9 miles all the way to US 276.
6	Turn right on US 276 and go just over a half a mile to turn right onto the other end of Sycamore Cove Trail.

| 7 | Stay on Sycamore Cove for 0.6 mile, then turn left up the short but steep trail that connects to Thrift Cove Trail above. |
| 8 | Turn left on Thrift Cove and return to the trailhead the way you came. |

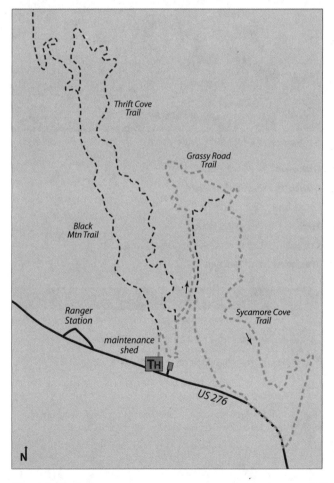

Headwaters Loop

A monument to the Civilian Conservation Corps stands at the trailhead.

Distance	9.8-mile loop
Difficulty	Easy to moderate
Location	Fish Hatchery
Time	1.5 to 2.5 hours
Crowds	Light weekdays, moderate weekends
Trailhead	Fish Hatchery

Route Directions	
1	Ride back out the way you drove in, cross the bridge, and turn left on FS 475.
2	Go just a short distance and turn right on FS 475B, a gravel road.
3	Reach Gumstand Gap 3.5 miles later. Turn left on FS 225.
4	Ride out and down the big hill for 0.9 mile and turn left around a gate onto Cove Creek Trail (yellow blazes).
5	In half a mile enter a campsite. Caney Bottom Loop Trail enters from the left here. Stay on Cove Creek Trail and begin a long, gradual descent.

6	After a couple of miles you'll notice Cove Creek Group Camp off to the left. Cross a tiny creek, turn left to head down to the group camp entrance road, and turn right.
7	When you reach the camp entrance, cross FS 475 and turn right on Davidson River Trail (blue blaze). It's just to the left of the small parking lot.
8	Ride above the river for 1.5 miles to the end of the trail. Turn right on FS 475 and continue back to the trailhead at the fish hatchery.

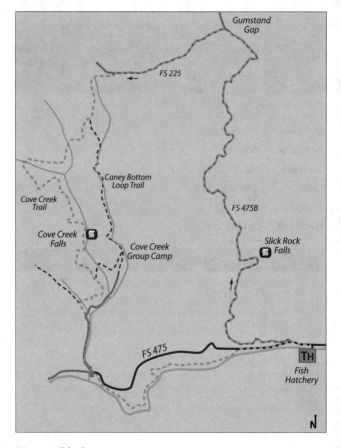

Most of Long Branch Trail is fast and fun.

Distance	8.4-mile loop
Difficulty	Moderate
Location	West of Fish Hatchery
Time	1.5 to 2.5 hours
Crowds	Light
Trailhead	Fish Hatchery

Route Directions	
	Note Portions of this route are on seasonal trails open to cyclists from October 15 to April 15 only.
1	Ride back out the way you drove in, cross the bridge, and turn left on FS 475.
2	After half a mile, turn left on Davidson River Trail (blue blaze).
3	Continue 1.4 miles and turn left back onto FS 475, which is now gravel.
4	You'll ride for 2.3 miles along the road to the gated entrance to Cemetery Loop. Continue 100 yards and turn left on Long Branch Trail (orange blaze).
5	In 0.8 mile, meet the other end of Cemetery Loop. Stay on Long Branch.

6	A mile later you'll cross gated FS 5095 and then 0.9 mile after that turn left on Butter Gap Trail (blue blaze).
7	It's all downhill now, and soon you'll pass through swampy Picklesimer Fields. At the end of this section, turn left on Cat Gap Loop Trail (orange blaze).
8	In half a mile cross a road and then a bridge. Not far beyond, you'll ride around the back side of the wildlife center. When you reach FS 475C, turn left to finish.

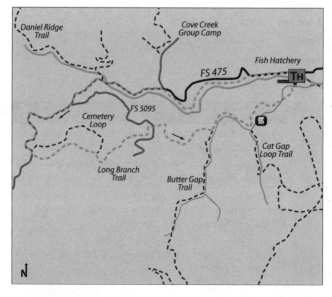

Toms Spring Falls

You'll ride past two waterfalls on this loop.

Distance	3-mile loop
Difficulty	Moderate
Location	West of Fish Hatchery
Time	45 minutes to 1.5 hours
Crowds	Light
Trailhead	Daniel Ridge

	Route Directions
1	Ride around the gate and cross the big bridge on Daniel Ridge Loop Trail (red blaze). When the trail splits beyond the bridge, go right toward the falls.
2	In 0.2 mile you'll pass the exit point of Daniel Ridge Loop Trail on your left; just beyond is Toms Spring Falls. Continue up FS 5046.
3	The road steadily climbs the ridge. After a little over a mile, look for a small stream to pass under the roadway. Stop here and walk up in the woods on the right to view Upper Toms Spring Branch Falls.
4	Just past the falls, turn left back onto Daniel Ridge Loop Trail to start a steep downhill with some big washout drops followed by several tricky bridges and some rooty, bumpy stretches.

5 Before you know it, you'll bottom out back beside Toms Spring Falls. Turn right and head down and across the bridge to finish the way you started.

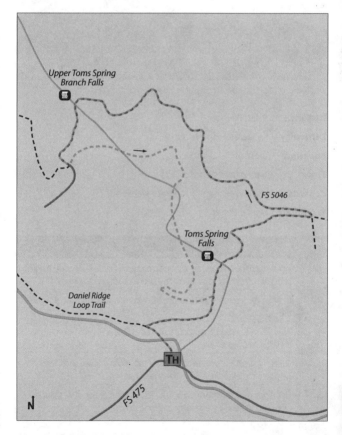

Daniel Ridge

Walk the bridge or ride through the creek—your choice.

Distance	4.1-mile loop
Difficulty	Moderate to strenuous
Location	West of Fish Hatchery
Time	1 to 2 hours
Crowds	Light weekdays, moderate weekends
Trailhead	Daniel Ridge

Route Directions	
1	Ride around the gate and across the big bridge on Daniel Ridge Loop Trail (red blaze). When the trail splits beyond the bridge go left, away from the falls.
2	In a mile you'll come to an old bridge site. Here the trail turns right, straight up the rocky hill.
3	After 0.3 mile of rugged climbing, turn right as Farlow Gap Trail enters from the left. Climb some more.
4	A half-mile later and you are at the top of the hill. An unmarked trail enters here from the left. Point it down the hill and hang on.
5	Half a mile down the hill cross FS 5046. This begins a section of washout drops, slippery bridges, and rooty, bumpy stretches.

| 6 | Before you know it, you'll bottom out just to the right of Toms Spring Falls. Turn right here to continue on the combined FS 5046 and the loop trail. |
| 7 | It's a half-mile back to the trailhead, just across the big bridge. |

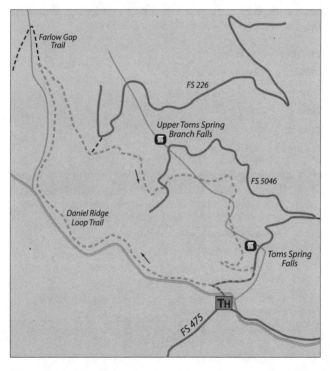

Cove Creek

Splashing through small creeks is the norm in Pisgah.

Distance	8-mile loop
Difficulty	Moderate to strenuous
Location	West of Fish Hatchery
Time	2.5 to 3.5 hours
Crowds	Light
Trailhead	Daniel Ridge

Route Directions	
1	Ride around the gate and across the big bridge on Daniel Ridge Loop Trail (red blaze). When the trail splits beyond the bridge, go right toward the falls.
2	In 0.2 mile you'll pass the exit point of Daniel Ridge Loop Trail on your left; just beyond is Toms Spring Falls. Continue up FS 5046.
3	At the first switchback on FS 5046, continue straight into the woods on an unmarked trail and head downhill immediately.
4	Reach a trail junction. Turn left here, down across a small creek and onto the Caney Bottom Loop Trail (blue blaze).
5	Just up ahead, stay straight at the split onto Cove Creek Trail (yellow blaze).

6	Several miles of gradual climbing later, you'll meet the other end of Caney Bottom Loop. Stay left here and ride out to FS 225 where you'll turn left.
7	Ride 0.3 mile to a where the road splits with a gate on each. Take the left gated road to stay on FS 225 to start a steady but gentle climb up the ridge.
8	Climb for about 2 miles as the road eventually becomes single track. At a bend, the roadway becomes completely grown over. Follow the well-worn but unmarked path on the left, down the hill.
9	This short trail deadends into Daniel Ridge Loop Trail. Turn left and follow it all the way back to the trailhead.

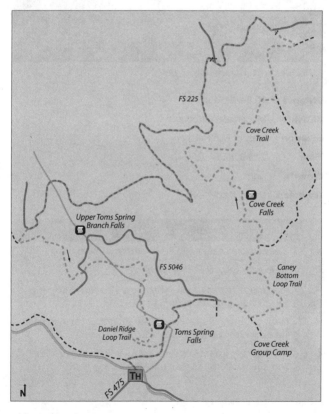

Butter Gap

You'll pass Grogan Creek Falls on Butter Gap Trail.

Distance	10.5-mile loop
Difficulty	Moderate to strenuous
Location	West of Fish Hatchery
Time	2 to 3 hours
Crowds	Light
Trailhead	Daniel Ridge

Route Directions	
1	Head west from the trailhead on FS 475 and climb to Gloucester Gap.
2	At Gloucester Gap after 2.2 miles, turn left on FS 471.
3	You'll climb a bit more on FS 471 and then begin a fast descent. Turn left at the second gated road on the left, FS 471D.
4	Climb again as the gated road becomes more like a trail. Up top, cross Art Loeb Trail and swing around to turn left on Butter Gap Trail (blue blaze).
5	From Butter Gap you'll ride a wicked downhill with lots of washout drops. After 1.2 miles of it, turn left on Long Branch Trail (orange blaze).

152   HIKING & MOUNTAIN BIKING PISGAH FOREST

| 6 | Climb a hill and cross a creek; soon you'll run into a gated forest road. This is FS 5095. Turn right and coast downhill several miles to FS 475. |
| 7 | Turn right on FS 475 and it's just a short distance back to the trailhead. |

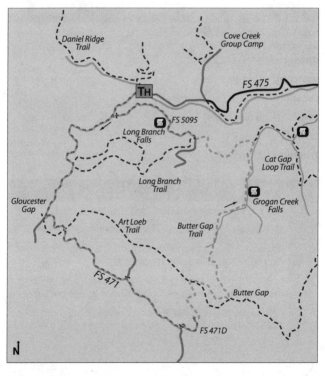

Farlow Gap Trail crosses the top of Shuck Ridge Creek Falls.

Distance	10.4-mile loop
Difficulty	Very strenuous
Location	West of Fish Hatchery
Time	3 to 4 hours
Crowds	Light
Trailhead	Daniel Ridge

Route Directions	
1	Head west from the trailhead on FS 475 and climb to Gloucester Gap.
2	At Gloucester Gap after 2.2 miles, turn right around the gate on FS 229.
3	After climbing 2.6 more miles, the road ends at a dirt barricade. Continue past the upper left barricade onto the old rocky roadbed.
4	Cross the Art Loeb Trail several more times up here; after 1.3 miles you'll reach Farlow Gap. Turn right for a steep downhill on Farlow Gap Trail (blue blaze).
5	The trail settles down somewhat after the first half-mile. After 2.5 miles, turn right down the steps on Daniel Ridge Loop Trail (red blaze).

| 6 | Follow Daniel Ridge Loop Trail over a steep and rocky descent, then bear left as it settles into an old roadbed which is a gradual downhill. |
| 7 | At the big bridge, turn right to ride back to the trailhead. |

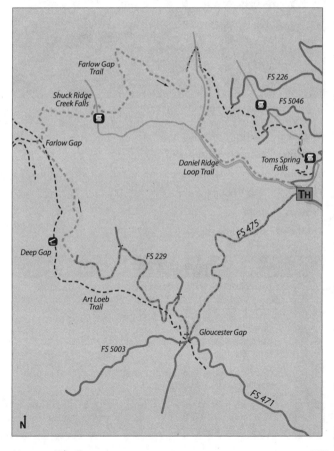

Buckhorn Gap

Negotiating these steps is a trick. Just don't try it on roller skates.

Distance	10.1-mile loop
Difficulty	Moderate to strenuous
Location	Avery Creek Watershed
Time	2 to 3 hours
Crowds	Light
Trailhead	Buckhorn Gap

Route Directions	
1	Ride back down FS 477 and turn left just past the horse rental stables onto FS 5058, a gated road.
2	Continue straight in another 1.0 miles as FS 5098 exits to the right.
3	2.8 miles further along, an unmarked road exits to the left in a switchback. Stay on FS 5058.
4	After another 0.6 mile of climbing you'll reach Buckhorn Gap; turn left up the steps on Black Mountain Trail (white blaze).
5	Climb up and over Rich Mountain along the ridgetop trail. When you reach Club Gap, turn left on Avery Creek Trail (blue blaze). Look for more washout drops as you head down this trail.

6   You'll descend another 2.0 miles down to where Buckhorn Gap Trail (yellow blaze) enters from the left over a footbridge. Turn right on Buckhorn Gap Trail here and follow it back to the trailhead.

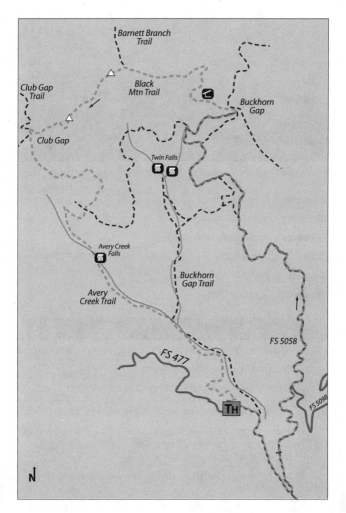

Bennett Gap

Looking Glass Rock is just to your right as you descend from Bennett Gap.

Distance	6.5-mile loop
Difficulty	Moderate to strenuous
Location	Avery Creek Watershed
Time	1 to 2 hours
Crowds	Light
Trailhead	Buckhorn Gap

Route Directions	
	Note Bennett Gap Trail is open to bicycles from October 15 to April 15 only.
1	Ride up the hill on FS 477 for almost 3 miles.
2	At the top of the climb, turn left on Bennett Gap Trail (red blaze).
3	Ride out the ridge for 0.4 mile to the clifftop view of Looking Glass Rock.
4	Continue down the mountain. In places it is steep; look out for washout drops that can come up fast. You'll pass turnoffs for Perry Cove Trail and Coontree Loop Trail as you descend.
5	After 2.3 miles you'll reach FS 477. Turn left here and ride less than a mile back to the trailhead.

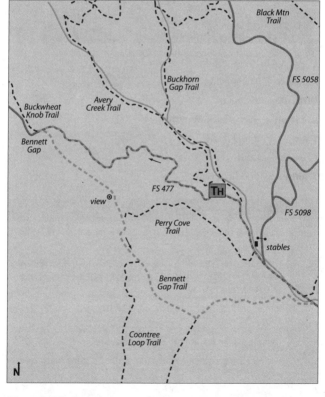

Black Mtn
Trail

FS 5058

Buckhorn
Gap Trail

Avery
Creek Trail

Buckwheat
Knob Trail

Bennett
Gap

FS 477

TH

view

FS 5098

Perry Cove
Trail

stables

Bennett
Gap Trail

Coontree
Loop Trail

N

Great views await from the cliffs atop Clawhammer Mountain.

Distance	11-mile loop
Difficulty	Strenuous
Location	Avery Creek Watershed
Time	2 to 3 hours
Crowds	Light
Trailhead	Buckhorn Gap

Route Directions	
1	Ride down Buckhorn Gap Trail (orange blaze) for a mile and cross the creek on a log bridge.
2	A little over a mile farther along, pass by the foot trail leading to Twin Falls. A half-mile beyond this, the trail splits. Take the right fork (left is for hikers only) which leads up to FS 5058.
3	Turn left on FS 5058 and ride it all the way to Buckhorn Gap.
4	At Buckhorn Gap, turn right on Black Mountain Trail (white blaze). The trail will get steep soon enough as it climbs to the cliffs above.
5	Another 1.2 miles up the mountain you'll reach the first of two clifftop views.

6	From the cliffs it's 1.5 miles of downhill bliss. Expect some big drops and washouts—and be on the lookout for folks coming up.
7	When you reach Pressley Gap, turn right on FS 5098 and continue downhill.
8	It's 2.4 miles to FS 5058; turn left to coast down to the stables.
9	Go right on FS 477 for the short ride up to the trailhead.

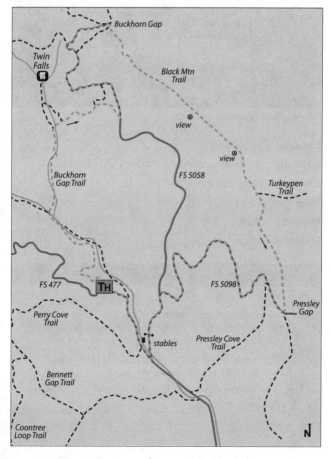

Bradley Creek flows swift and cold.

Distance	7-mile loop
Difficulty	Moderate to strenuous
Location	Along FS Route 1206
Time	1.5 to 2.5 hours
Crowds	Light
Trailhead	Yellow Gap

Route Directions	
1	Ride west on FS 1206 down the hill to the first roadside campsites on the left.
2	Drop down to the campsites by the creek and turn left, following the left shore of Bradley Creek on Bradley Creek Trail (orange blaze). It does not see much use, so be prepared for some blowdown debris.
3	After a long 1.5 miles down the creek, you'll come to a dam backing up a small reservoir; the creek crossings are almost over.
4	Just 0.1 mile farther on, turn left at a timber cut onto FS 5015. It most likely will not be marked.
5	A 4-mile steady climb brings you back to the trailhead at Yellow Gap.

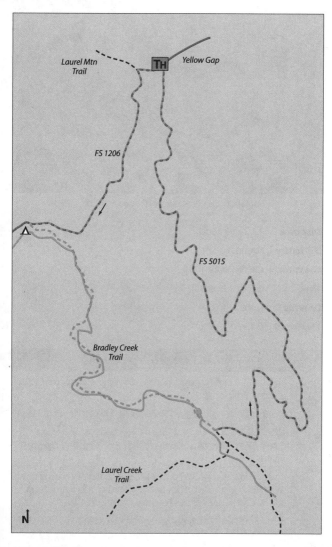

Horse Cove Gap

You'll keep your feet dry as you cross South Mills River on bridges.

Distance	12.2-mile loop
Difficulty	Strenuous
Location	Off FS Route 1206
Time	2.5 to 4 hours
Crowds	Light
Trailhead	Gauging Station

	Route Directions
1	Ride back up the road you drove in on for half a mile and turn right on FS 5018 to begin a steady climb.
2	After 3.8 miles, reach the end of FS 5018. Continue straight onto Horse Cove Gap Trail (red blaze).
3	A steep 0.5-mile downhill brings you to Horse Cove Gap. Turn right here on Squirrel Gap Trail (blue blaze).
4	Wind around on Squirrel Gap Trail for 2.4 miles, finally dropping down to cross South Mills River on a long suspension bridge. Continue from here on South Mills River Trail (white blaze). You'll climb up, away from the river.
5	Almost 3 miles later, turn right as Buckhorn Gap Trail enters from the left.

6 | Ride down the hill and cross the river again, this time on a concrete bridge. Continue another mile beside the river, back to the trailhead.

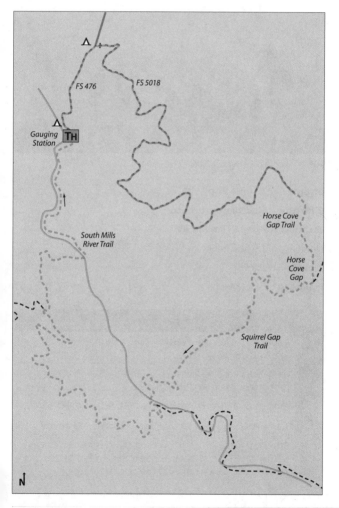

Pilot Cove–Slate Rock

Ride right across the top of Slate Rock.

Distance	7.1-mile loop
Difficulty	Moderate to strenuous
Location	Along FS Route 1206
Time	1.5 to 3 hours
Crowds	Light
Trailhead	Pilot Cove

Route Directions
1	Ride east on FS 1206 down the hill for 1.7 miles and turn left on Pilot Cove/ Slate Rock Creek Trail (blue blaze).
2	For the next 3.0 miles you'll climb steadily uphill above Slate Rock Creek, passing two waterfalls along the way to the gap.
3	At the gap, turn left to climb some more on Pilot Cove Loop Trail (yellow blaze).
4	In another 0.9 mile, you'll roll out onto Slate Rock. Stop here for the view.
5	From Slate Rock the trail turns much more steeply down the mountain. Continue another 1.3 miles to connect with the other side of the Pilot Cove/ Slate Rock Creek Trail. Turn left and it's 0.2 mile back to the trailhead.

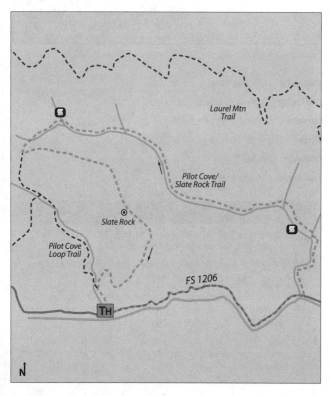

Laurel Mtn
Trail

Pilot Cove/
Slate Rock Trail

Slate Rock

Pilot Cove
Loop Trail

FS 1206

TH

N

Laurel Mountain

There are a lot of big drops coming down Pilot Mountain Trail.

Distance	15-mile loop
Difficulty	Very strenuous
Location	Along FS Route 1206
Time	3 to 4 hours
Crowds	Light
Trailhead	Yellow Gap

Route Directions	
1	Ride across the road and uphill on Laurel Mountain Trail (blue blaze). You'll climb steadily for the 6.6 miles. Toward the top are several very steep pitches.
2	At 6.4 miles, reach Turkey Spring Gap. Here is your first marked trail junction. Turn left on Laurel Mountain Connector Trail (yellow blaze).
3	After another 0.2 mile of uphill, it's time to head down. Turn left on Pilot Rock Trail (orange blaze). You'll descend now for 2.4 miles through numerous tight switchbacks and over multiple big drops.
4	Just as things are beginning to settle down, the trail crosses an old logging road. You may notice a lightly used campsite on the right. Turn left here on this unmarked road.

5	Ride 0.5 mile on this old road as it gently climbs back up the ridge; ignore an old road coming in from the right. Eventually you will intersect with Pilot Cove/Slate Rock Creek Trail (blue blaze). Turn left on it.
6	Climb 0.2 mile to an intersection with Pilot Cove Loop Trail. Continue straight to begin a 3-mile descent.
7	Reach FS 1206 after passing several waterfalls along the way. Turn left, coast down the hill, and then climb back up to Yellow Gap to finish.

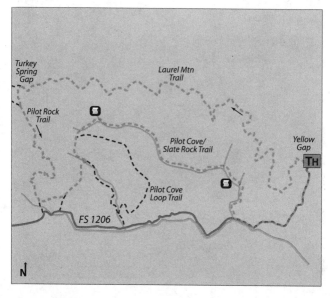

Pisgah Forest

Waterfalls

Waterfalls are one of the main attractions in Pisgah Forest. You're likely to encounter at least one wanderer with a pamphlet or brochure in hand searching for a particular fall. Some will come with expensive camera equipment, others with a swimsuit; almost all have a desire to experience that uplift you feel while standing in the spray of a cascade. Many of the hikes and bike rides listed in this book will take you past one or more waterfalls. In fact, sometimes there's no better way to see a waterfall than going for a day hike, an overnight hike, or a bike ride.

Unfortunately, every year foolish behavior causes people to die at waterfalls. People have died at some of the waterfalls listed in this book. Here's what usually happens. They try to climb the cliff or steep slope beside a waterfall to get a better view or take a picture or reach the top, and then they slip and fall. They try to peer over the edge at the top, and then they slip and fall. They try to climb the waterfall itself, and then they slip and fall. Everything near a waterfall—rocks, roots, fallen trees—is wet and slippery. If you do any of these things, it's only a matter of time before you slip and fall, too. At best you'll twist an ankle or break an arm, at worst it could be fatal. Certainly your foolish mistake will ruin what could have been a nice outing for you and everyone else. *Always exercise extreme caution and common sense around waterfalls.*

Looking Glass Falls

Looking Glass is probably Pisgah's most well known falls; the fact that it is right beside US 276 probably helps. This block-style waterfall drops approximately 60 feet into a shallow pool.

Directions From the ranger station drive north on US 276 for 5.6 miles. There's parking along the road and a steep staircase leads down to the base.

Cedar Rock Creek Falls

You'll need to hike a little ways to see this waterfall. This horsetail-style falls is about 20 feet high and makes for a nice destination; it's less than a mile from the trailhead. You'll pass near it on the *Cat Gap Loop* hike (p. 58).

Directions From the ranger station, drive north on US 276 for 3.7 miles. Turn left toward Pisgah Fish Hatchery and Wildlife Education Center and drive 1.5 miles. The trailhead is at the fish hatchery. From the back of the parking lot, just past the Wildlife Education Center, go around the gate and turn right on Cat Gap Loop Trail. After crossing Cedar Rock Creek on a bridge and then a road, continue 10 to 15 minutes more and look for an unmarked side trail on the left. Take this trail to the falls, which you can hear before you see.

Cedar Rock Creek Falls.

Grogan Creek Falls

Grogan Creek Falls is close enough to Cedar Rock Falls to at least consider seeing both in the same hike. It's about a mile farther, just off of Butter Gap Trail. This distinctive tiered waterfall drops about 20 feet over a stairstep boulder. You'll pass near this waterfall on the *Butter Gap* hike (p. 84) and bike ride (p. 152).

Directions Follow the directions for Cedar Rock Creek as above. Stay on Cat Gap Loop Trail until it intersects with Butter Gap Trail. Turn right on Butter Gap, passing the intersection with Long Bottom Trail until you reach the falls on your left. You can't miss it.

Slickrock Falls

This is another one of the easy-access waterfalls. Located right off gravel FS Route 475B, it is best after periods of wet weather. You'll pass this 30-foot, tiered, plunge-style waterfall on the *Headwaters Loop* bike ride (p. 142).

Directions From the ranger station, drive north on US 276 for 3.7 miles. Turn left toward Pisgah Fish Hatchery and Wildlife Education Center and drive 1.5 miles. Just past the fish hatchery, turn right onto gravel FS 475B. After about a mile, look for a pulloff on the right where 475B makes a sharp turn to the left. Once out of your car, you can hear the falls. Head for the information board and follow the short trail up to the falls.

Cove Creek Falls

This is a big and exciting waterfall and getting to it involves a 2.6-mile round-trip hike. You can view its 80-foot, multi-tiered drop from the bottom by taking a steep side trail down to the big plungepool. The *Caney Bottom Loop* (p. 60) and *Caney Bottom* (p. 94) hikes will take you to this falls, and so will the *Headwaters* (p. 142) and *Cove Creek* (p. 150) bike rides.

Directions From the ranger station, drive north on US 276 for 3.7 miles. Turn left toward Pisgah Fish Hatchery and Wildlife Education Center and drive 4.7 miles to where the pavement ends at the entrance to Cove Creek Group Camp. Park at the small lot across from the entrance. Walk past the gate on the entrance road to the campground and follow the road for a half-mile or so. Just before the group camp, turn left on Caney Bottom Loop. Follow it for another half-mile and bear left on Cove Creek Trail. In yet another half-mile, look for a "falls" sign on the right indicating the side trail down to the base of Cove Creek Falls.

Cove Creek Falls.

Toms Spring Falls

It's only a short walk up to the base of this tall waterfall, which drops right down the cliff face in various tiers and is over 100 feet high. The *Daniel Ridge Loop* (p. 62) and *Butter Gap–Cove Creek* (p. 86) hikes pass by this falls, as do the *Toms Spring Falls* (p. 146) and *Cove Creek* (p. 150) bike rides.

Directions From the ranger station, drive north on US 276 for 3.7 miles. Turn left toward Pisgah Fish Hatchery and Wildlife Education Center and drive 4.7 miles to where the pavement ends at the entrance to Cove Creek Group Camp. Continue onto the gravel road straight ahead for another mile to the parking area on the right. The trail starts by passing around the gate and across the wide bridge. Just past the bridge, bear right as the trail splits; just a short distance up the hill you'll come to the falls on your left.

Upper Toms Spring Branch Falls

You have to be a little more ambitious to get to this waterfall; it's about 1.5 miles past Toms Spring Falls on the same old logging road. With a drop of around 30 feet it's not as high, but it sees far fewer visitors. You'll pass it on the *Daniel Ridge Loop* hike (p. 62) and the *Toms Spring Falls* bike ride (p. 146).

Directions From the ranger station, drive north on US 276 for 3.7 miles. Turn left toward Pisgah Fish Hatchery and Wildlife Education Center and drive 4.7 miles to where the pavement ends at the entrance to Cove Creek Group Camp. Continue onto the gravel road straight ahead for another mile to the parking area on the right. The trail starts by passing around the gate and across the wide bridge. Just past the bridge, bear right as the trail splits. Soon you'll pass Toms Spring Falls on the left. Continue up the road for 40 minutes or so. You'll hear the waterfall off to the right as the road crosses a small creek. Follow the short trail up to the base.

Shuck Ridge Creek Falls

One of the more remote waterfalls in Pisgah located on a trail, you might best view this one while mountain biking the *Farlow Gap* ride (p. 154) or backpacking the *Deep Gap* hike (p. 90). Otherwise, plan on an all-day hike to see it. No matter how you go, the falls is quite pretty with its secluded plungepool. The trail crosses the very top of the falls.

Directions From the ranger station, drive north on US 276 for 3.7 miles. Turn left toward Pisgah Fish Hatchery and Wildlife Education Center and drive 4.7 miles to where the pavement ends at the entrance to Cove Creek Group Camp. Continue onto the gravel road straight ahead for another mile to the parking area on the right. The trail starts by going around the gate and across the wide bridge. After the bridge, turn left on Daniel Ridge Trail and follow it for about 2 miles. Turn left (after a steep climb) onto Farlow Gap Trail. It's another 2.3 miles up the mountain and along the sides of the ridge to the top of the waterfall.

Long Branch Falls

A relatively short walk up a gated forest service road and then a scramble up an unmarked trail will get you to this falls. It drops in multiple 15-foot tiers of angled rock before disappearing into the rhododendron.

Directions From the ranger station, drive north on US 276 for 3.7 miles. Turn left toward Pisgah Fish Hatchery and Wildlife Education Center and drive 4.7 miles to where the pavement ends at the entrance to Cove Creek Group Camp. Continue onto the gravel road straight ahead for another mile, passing the parking area on the right for Daniel Ridge, and onward a little farther to the gated FS 5095 on the left. Park here, making sure not to block the gate. Walk around the gate and up the road about a mile to the first creek crossing. Just before reaching the creek, look for an unmarked trail on the right scrambling up the hill. Follow this a short distance to view the falls.

Courthouse Falls

Getting to this waterfall means a long drive on a gravel road, but it's time well spent. Courthouse Falls drops 45 feet into a deep crystal-clear plungepool. It's a classic horsetail-style waterfall.

Directions From the ranger station, drive south out of the forest to the first traffic light in the town of Pisgah Forest. Turn right on US 64 and continue through the town of Brevard to the intersection of NC 215. Turn right and head north on NC 215 for 10.2 miles to turn right on FS 140. Continue another 3 miles and park just past the bridge over Courthouse Creek. Look for Courthouse Falls Trail (formerly Summey Cove Trail) on the left side of the road. Follow it downstream for about 10 minutes to reach the falls.

Chestnut Falls

If you're visiting Courthouse Falls, you might want to go to Chestnut as well. It's about a mile hike up to the falls on a gated road. The falls drops 20 feet or so over large boulders.

Directions Follow the directions to FS 140 as above for Courthouse Falls. Once on FS 140, drive 2.7 miles to gated FS 5031 on the right. Park here and walk up this road about a mile. Just before the road splits, look for a path on the right heading down to the base of the falls. You'll hear it before you see it.

Moore Cove Falls

This waterfall is almost as popular as Looking Glass Falls, so expect a crowd in high season. A short trail leads right off US 276 up to a viewing platform near the base of the 50-foot falls. It's a classic plunge waterfall, dropping onto a jumble of boulders.

Moore Cove Falls.

Directions From the ranger station, drive north on US 276 for 6.7 miles to a roadside parking area on the right. Follow the trail 0.75 mile to the base of the falls.

Avery Creek Falls

The best way to see this waterfall is either on the overnight *Buckhorn Gap Shelter* hike (p. 98) or on the *Buckhorn Gap* mountain bike ride (p. 156). If you make a special day hike just to see it, note that it is best seen from the trail above it at a distance of about 100 yards.

Directions From the ranger station, drive north on US 276 for a little less than a mile and turn right on Avery Creek Road (FS 477). Continue past White Pines Group Camp and after another 1.5 miles pass the horseback riding concession area. Continue another 0.4 mile to park at the Buckhorn Gap trailhead on the right. From here walk out Buckhorn Gap Trail for a mile or so. When you reach the creek, turn left on Avery Creek Trail. Continue up the hill another half-mile. You'll hear and see the waterfall crashing down through the rhododendron on your right.

Twin Falls.

Twin Falls

Here are two waterfalls for the price of one. Walk up to Twin Falls and you'll see them side by side, about 50 feet from one another. A map and directions for the *Twin Falls* hike are on p. 178.

High Falls

This is the only waterfall on South Mills River. At just 15 feet, it's not even close to the highest in Pisgah. Still, it's a beautiful waterfall on a sizable stream, and there's a huge swimming hole at the bottom. The hike in is challenging.

Directions From the ranger station, drive north on US 276 for 12 miles. Just north of the Pink Beds, turn right on FS 1206. Drive about 3 miles and turn right on FS 476. Follow this road to where it ends at a gate, parking area, and campsites. Walk around the gate onto South Mills River Trail and follow it for 1.5 miles. When South Mills River Trail crosses the river on an old concrete bridge (don't cross this bridge), look for an unmarked trail on the left. Follow this trail along the river for a half-mile or so, cross (i.e., wade) the river, and continue about a quarter-mile more to the falls. Note that this trail is not maintained and at times the going could be rough.

Sliding Rock Falls

The most popular swimming hole in Pisgah, if not all of Western North Carolina. Sliding Rock is a 60-foot natural waterslide visited by hundreds of people each day in the heat of summer. A fee is charged and, yes, there are lifeguards.

Directions From the ranger station, drive north on US 276 for 8 miles. You can't miss the huge parking area on the right.

Log Hollow Branch Falls

With a little extra exploration, you can actually see four waterfalls (three are unnamed) on this excursion to Log Hollow Branch Falls. Two are right on the road/trail and two are not far off it. The falls are quite impressive, ranging in height from 30 to 80 feet.

Directions From the ranger station, drive north on US 276 for 10 miles and turn left on FS 475B. Continue down this road for 1.6 miles to a hairpin turn. Look for gated FS 5043 on your right. Park here, walk around the gate, and head up the road. After about 400 yards you'll come to the first bridge. Look for an unmarked trail heading up the right side of the creek. Follow it 400 more yards to a 60-foot unnamed waterfall (#1). Back at the first bridge, continue up FS 5043 a short distance to the next bridge; here you'll see Log Hollow Branch Falls (#2). Look for a faint trail heading up the hill to the left of this waterfall. It leads, in a few hundred yards, to an unnamed upper waterfall on the same creek (#3); it's a scramble to get to this one. From the second bridge on FS 5043, continue up the road another ten minutes or so to find an 80-foot waterfall right beside the road (#4).

Skinny Dip Falls

Don't get your hopes up. So many people visit this waterfall that it's not really secluded enough for skinny dipping. However, it *is* a great spot for jumping off a rock into a deep pool. If you're hiking the *Mountains-to-Sea Trail* (p. 108), you'll pass right by this waterfall.

Directions From the ranger station, drive north on US 276 up to the Blue Ridge Parkway. Turn right, continue to milepost 417, and park at the Looking Glass Rock overlook. On hot sunny days, this parking lot is full of folks heading down to the waterfall. Walk across the road and bear left onto the Mountains-to-Sea Trail. It's about a half-mile down to the falls.

Second Falls Yellowstone Prong.

Second Falls on Yellowstone Prong

A long series of wooden steps leads to the base of this popular waterfall in Graveyard Fields. At 55 feet, it's the easiest to access of the three falls on Yellowstone Prong. You can view this falls on the *Graveyard Fields* hike (p. 72).

Directions From the ranger station, drive north on US 276 up to the Blue Ridge Parkway. Turn left on the Parkway and continue to the Graveyard Fields parking area on the right; it's huge. From the parking lot, take the northernmost steps (the ones on the right as you face away from the Parkway) down, to cross a bridge over Yellowstone Prong. At this point you are at the lip of the falls. Beyond the bridge take a right and continue down the wooden steps on the short trail, winding your way to the falls' base.

Upper Falls on Yellowstone Prong

The scenic hike to Upper Falls takes you through the heart of Graveyard Fields. This 40-foot waterfall drops over a cliff face and then through several sluices. You can view it on the *Graveyard Fields* hike (p. 72).

Directions Drive up to Graveyard Fields as described above. From the parking lot take the southernmost steps (those to the left as you face away from the Parkway). Follow this trail to cross Yellowstone Prong. Then bear left (upstream) on Upper Falls Trail, which leads you to the base of the falls. All told it's about 1.5 miles to the falls, and navigating the trails can be a bit tricky. Just be sure you're heading upstream on the opposite side of the stream from the Parkway, and you should be fine.

Wildcat Falls

You'll find this waterfall on the far western side of Pisgah, not far above NC 215. The neat thing about it is that you'll cross right over the central section of the waterfall via a concrete bridge on Flat Laurel Creek Trail. It's about 60 feet high, cascading over a cliff on the upper side of the bridge and down through several sluices on the lower side.

Directions From the ranger station, head north on US 276 up to the Blue Ridge Parkway. Turn left on the Parkway and continue to its intersection with NC 215. Turn right (north—and actually a left turn off the exit ramp) on NC 215 and go another 0.8 mile. Park at the small campsite on the right side of the road. Walk around the gate, down, and across the creek on Flat Laurel Creek Trail. In about 0.75 mile you'll come to the waterfall where the concrete bridge crosses the creek.

Appendices

Appendix A Management Resources

Pisgah National Forest–Pisgah District
1600 Pisgah Hwy
Pisgah Forest, NC 28768
828-877-3265
fs.usda.gov/nfsnc

Blue Ridge Parkway
199 Hemphill Knob Rd
Asheville, NC 28803
828-298-0398
nps.gov/blri

North Carolina Wildlife Resources Commission
1751 Varsity Dr
Raleigh, NC 27606
919-707-0050
ncwildlife.org

Appendix B Local Outfitters & Bike Shops

WNC Outfitters

Black Dome Mountain Sports
140 Tunnel Rd
Asheville, NC 28805
828-251-2001

Blackrock Outdoor Company
570 W Main St
Sylva, NC 28779
828-631-4453

Diamond Brand Outdoors
1378 Hendersonville Rd
Asheville, NC 28803
828-684-6262

53 Biltmore Ave
Asheville, NC 28801
828-771-4761

REI Asheville
Biltmore Park Town Square
31 Schenck Pkwy
Asheville, NC 28803
828-687-0918

The Frugal Backpacker
52 Westgate Pkwy
Asheville, NC 28806
828-209-1530

WNC Bike Shops

Pisgah Forest

Sycamore Cycles
112 Hendersonville Hwy
Pisgah Forest, NC 28768
828-877-5790

The Hub
49 Pisgah Hwy #60
Pisgah Forest, NC 28768
828-884-8670

Asheville

Asheville Bicycle Company
1000 Merrimon Ave
Asheville, NC 28804
828-254-2771

Beer City Bicycles
144 Biltmore Ave
Asheville, NC 28801
828-575-2453

Billy Goat Bicycles
5 Regent Park Blvd #106
Asheville, NC 28806
828-525-2460

Carolina Fatz
1240 Brevard Rd #3
Asheville, NC 28806
828-665-7744

Epic Cycles
800 Haywood Rd
Asheville, NC 28806
828-505-4455

Hearn Cycling
28 Asheland Ave
Asheville, NC 28801
828-253-4800

Liberty Bicycles
1378 Hendersonville Rd
Asheville, NC 28803
828-274-2453

Motion Makers Cycles
878 Brevard Rd
Asheville, NC 28806
828-633-2227

Youngblood Bicycles
233 Merrimon Ave
Asheville, NC 28801
282-251-4686

Hendersonville

Sycamore Cycles
146 3rd Ave
Hendersonville, NC 28792
828-693-1776

The Bicycle Company
779 N Church St #A
Hendersonville, NC 28792
828-969-1500

Waynesville

Rolls Rite Bicycles
1362 Asheville Rd

Waynesville, NC 28786
828-276-6080

Sylva

Motion Makers Cycles
36 Allen St
Sylva, NC 28779
828-586-6925

Bryson City

Bryson City Bicycles
157 Everett St
Bryson City, NC 28713
828-488-1988

Tsali Cycles
35 Slope St
Bryson City, NC 28713
828-488-9010

Upstate South Carolina Outfitter & Bike Shops

Travelers Rest

Sunrift Adventures
1 Center St
Travelers Rest, SC 29690
864-834-3019

Greenville

Appalachian Outfitters
191 Halton Rd
Greenville, SC 29607
864-987-0618

Carolina Triathlon
928 S Main St
Greenville, SC 29601
864-331-8483

Half Moon Outfitters
1420 Laurens Rd
Greenville, SC 29607
864-233-4001

REI Greenville
The Point
1140 Woodruff Rd #400
Greenville, SC 29607
864-297-0588

Sunshine Cycles
1826 N Pleasantburg Dr
Greenville, SC 29609
864-244-2925

Trek Store South Carolina
1426 Laurens Rd
Greenville, SC 29607
864-235-8320

TTR Bikes
101 S Hudson St
Greenville, SC 29601
864-283-6401

Spartanburg

Bike Worx
1321 Union St
Spartanburg, SC 29302
864-542-2453

The Local Hiker
173 E Main St
Spartanburg, SC 29306
864-764-1651

Trek Store South Carolina
105 Franklin Ave
Spartanburg, SC 29301
864-574-5373

Pickens

Southern Appalachian Outdoors
506 W Main Street
Pickens, SC 29671
864-507-2195

Clemson

Elkmont Trading Company
100 Liberty Dr
Clemson, SC 29631
864-653-7002

Anderson

Grady's Great Outdoors
3440 Clemson Blvd
Anderson, SC 29621
864-226-5283

Trek Store South Carolina
2714 N Main St
Anderson, SC 29621
864-226-4579

Milestone Press

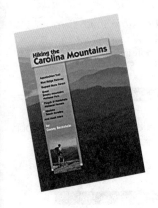

Hiking

- *Backpacking Overnights: NC Mountains, SC Upstate* by Jim Parham

- *Day Hiking the North Georgia Mountains* by Jim Parham

- *Hiking Atlanta's Hidden Forests* by Jonah McDonald

- *Hiking North Carolina's Blue Ridge Mountains* by Danny Bernstein

- *Hiking the Carolina Mountains* by Danny Bernstein

- *Family Hikes in Upstate South Carolina* by Scott Lynch

- *Waterfalls Hikes of North Georgia* by Jim Parham

- *Waterfalls Hikes of Upstate South Carolina* by Thomas E. King

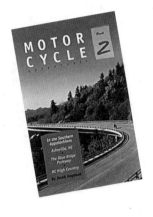

Motorcycle Adventure Series
by Hawk Hagebak

- *1–Southern Appalachians:
  North GA, East TN,
  Western NC*

- *2–Southern Appalachians:
  Asheville NC,
  Blue Ridge Parkway,
  NC High Country*

- *3–Central Appalachians:
  Virginia's Blue Ridge,
  Shenandoah Valley,
  West Virginia Highlands*

Mountain Bike Guides
by Jim Parham

- *Mountain Bike Trails—
  NC Mountains &
  SC Upstate*

- *Mountain Bike Trails—
  North GA &
  Southeast TN*

Milestone Press

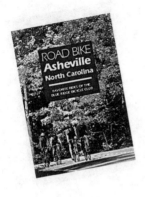

Road Bike Guide Series

- *Road Bike Asheville, NC* by the Blue Ridge Bicycle Club

- *Road Bike North Georgia* by Jim Parham

- *Road Bike the Smokies* by Jim Parham

Family Adventure

- *Natural Adventures in the Mountains of North Georgia* by Jim Parham & Mary Ellen Hammond

Pocket Guides

- *Hiking South Carolina's Foothills Trail* by Scott Lynch

- *Hiking & Mountain Biking DuPont State Forest* by Scott Lynch

- *Hiking & Mountain Biking Pisgah Forest* by Jim Parham

Wildflower Guides

- *Wildflower Walks & Hikes: North Carolina Mountains* by Jim Parham

Can't find the Milestone Press guidebook you want at a bookseller near you? Call us at 828-488-6601 or visit milestonepress.com for purchase information.

About the Author

Since publishing his first mountain bike trail guide in 1992, Jim Parham has written more than a dozen adventure guidebooks for hiking, backpacking, mountain biking, and road biking in the Southeast, and drawn his signature maps for numerous guides by other authors. A native North Carolinian who grew up in north Georgia and lived for years in east Tennessee, he now resides on the North Carolina side of the Great Smoky Mountains.